My Faith: A Cameroon to be renewed

Les Editions Veritas

Collection éducation
Collection economia
Collection du Savoir
Collection Livres religieux

©Copyrigths Editions Veritas, 2011

Place de la Cathédrale, BP. 179 Douala

Webside : www.macacosnet.com

E-mail: editionsveritas@yahoo.fr

ISBN:9956-635-07-3

Collection of Religious Books

Cardinal Christian TUMI

My Faith : A Cameroon to be renewed

English edition

The author

* *The politiccal regimes of Ahmadou Ahidjo and Paul Biya, and Christian Tumi, Priest*, Douala, Macacos, 2006.

* *Pocket Catechism of the Catholic Church*, Frigento, Casa Maria Editrice, 2007.

Contents

Preface

Through the publication of this book entitled: MY FAITH: A CAMEROON TO BE RENEWED - His Eminence Christian Cardinal TUMI, the retired Archbishop of Douala, continues his fight of a man of faith.

His retirement gives him more time either to conclude his fight for justice and peace or to undertake another project for the renewal of our society.

That is why in this reflection the Cardinal shares with us what should be done for Cameroon to be renewed; practical change is impossible without the ethical and spiritual conversion of Cameroonians. If not realized, Cameroon will lose its identity as a nation.

True to his incisive and frank style, the author does not conceal his English and French cultural heritage. The Anglo-saxon trait reveals itself in the forceful cry of Martin Luther KING, *"I have a dream"* of the sixties prophesying the future and the multiracial harmony in the U.S.A. which was still under the yoke of racial discrimination. The author's acquaintance with the French culture also recalls the prophetic dream of Victor HUGO. He breathes the unpleasant air of the future and already embraces the handsome child yet to be born... it suffices for the author in given conditions, to grasp the reality of the new world built on solidarity and founded on love of neighbour :

A child dreams, a child dreams ...
He does well to dream dreams ;
He does well to dream dreams ;
Full of daimond
Suns of flames
And beautiful ladies
Who have souls
A dream that delights ;
He sees streams,
A voice that sings
Comes but from the bottom of the waters
Her sisters are more beautiful
Her father is near her,
Her mother has wings,
Like birds. [V. HUGO] (author's translation)

As a Christian and a synod father with a wealth of experience, Cardinal Tumi does not have any fear of being contradicted. Furthermore, he is well aquainted with the 57 resolutions of the 2nd assembly of the synod of Bishops for Africa held in Rome in October 2009. The synod placed great emphasis on the importance of the application of the social teachings of the Church in Africa.

Cardinal Tumi has further developed the synod message to suit the Cameroon situation given that he relates very well with people from all walks of life and who belong in various social groups. He is certain that by adopting the social teaching of the church, Cameroon stands to benefit. If we accept that Cameroon was a prosperous country, isn't it possible to regain her lost integrity? Cardinal TUMI turns to the recent past of our country which for him is the. cause of our socio-political degeneration; the dreadful administration of the common good, separation between the English and the French speaking Cameroonians, the lack of respect for the human person, corruption in the legal profession, moral corruption and trust in superstitious practices in public life under cover of separation of Church and State (Secularism). In the last analysis the Cardinal asks himself if these immoral practices are not a revival of the immoral past!

Chapters 5, 6, and 7 of the book express vividly Cardinal TUMI's dream of a new Cameroon. The problem of national unity and prosperity of the country is discussed and the author believes that without God, we can do nothing worth while:

> If the Lord does not build the house,
> The work of the builders is useless,
> If the Lord does not protect the city,
> in vain does its gard keep watch... (Ps 126/127)

The terminology borrowed from HEIDEGER helps towards a better understanding of the social situation of our country as expressed by the Cardinal.

If Cameroon emerged on a solid foundation, then our recent past shows that because of our lack of ethics and practical truth, that foundation has been fundamentally weakened. Our national edifice has crumbled under the strain of secularism. The celebration of 50 years of independence and unification should offer us a new spring board on which to take off.

As far as this second phase of nation building is concerned, King David's example in the Bible can be a model and guide for our politicians and for all citizens. Because of his fidelity and loyalty, God granted him prosperity, security, and national and international popularity. As long as the people of Israel put their trust in God, they felt quite secured and at peace. From the moment they turned away from God their misfortune started. The Cardinal's reaction to such a situation is that all those who believe in God should awaken their conscience ethically. From chapter 8 to 12. His Eminence Christian Cardinal TUMI discusses his views from various aspects on the way towards the renewal of Cameroon. The issues put forth are thought-provocking as they are meant to awaken our conscience. Among these is the division between the English speaking and French speaking Cameroonians English and French as foreign languages, should not serve as instruments of ideology of colonial conquest.

The author invites us to be vigilant and responsable and never let other people tell us what our future should be, as it was the case in our colonial history. The renewal of our country can neither be given to an oligarchy nor to a monarchy, be it essentially Anglophone or francophone ; were this the case, any of the two would confiscate power for personal or egoistic interests. In his appeal for a new heart, the Cardinal hopes Cameroon can be transformed.

MAY HIS VOICE BE HEEDED TO
Mgr Victor TONYE BAKOT.

Foreword

The great honor that Christian Cardinal TUMI has given me to write the foreword of this book   invites me to react with simplicity, and without pretending to give any orientation to the reader, nor to deal with the thought of the writer.

Cardinal Christian TUMI follows very closely the political life of Cameroon and makes that known when necessary. Because of this, many have thought that he has the intention of becoming the president of Cameroon.

But what is surprising and that was not expected is the title of his book *"My Faith: a Cameroon to be renewed"*. In this title the credo, the faith of the priest of the Catholic church is demonstrated as he points out the way forward which is the transformation of our country into a nation well administered and governed and where its inhabitants live in harmony and mutual respect conscious of their obligations to each other.

All the same it should be recalled that Cardinal TUMI is a Christian in the Catholic church " in the world of today", a Bishop in a church that has been renewed by the 2nd Vatican Council, which teaches that the kingdom of God is built in and by profane activities. It was Pope Paul V1 who continued and closed the council opened by Pope John XXIII, who, in his " profession of faith of the people of God," said:

I gave the impulse of living like a Christian : "…. **We confess that the Kingdom of God began here below in the Church of Christ is not of this world whose form is passing, and that its proper growth cannot be confounded with the progress of civilization, of science or of human technology, but that it consists in an ever more profound knowledge of the unfathomable riches of Christ, an ever stronger hope in eternal blessings, an ever more ardent response to the love of God, and an ever more generous bestowal of grace and holiness among men. But it is this same love which induces the Church to concern herself constantly about the true temporal welfare of men. Without ceasing to recall to her children that they have not here a lasting dwelling, she also urges them to contribute, each according to his vocation and his means, to the welfare of their earthly city, to promote justice, peace and brotherhood among men, to give their aid freely to their brothers, especially to the poorest and most unfortunate. …"**

Therefore if the people of God in Cameroon did not yet know, now they will learn by a living example and by the most authoritative voice that, the organization of our country, the cradle of our ancestors, according to the will of God, is the work that God has given them. For a Christian, the reception of the sacraments is the means which helps us to accomplish this work.

Another lesson to be learnt from reading the Cardinal's book is to put in practice the social teaching of the church. To every difficult social situation which is a handicap to the renewal of our country, there is a corresponding teaching or orientation that the church gives that helps overcome such an obstacle or situation. The church therefore has some thing good to offer to the world which is often ignored. As a francophone Cameroonian reading his book, I think that the Cardinal considers the historical event of unification as an Anglophone and that is good, for two reasons:

1- He feels and thinks like an Anglophone when he expresses himself with the liberty of the child of God. Because of this, the francophone Cameroonian on the street, understands why our compatriots, the members of the Southern Cameroon National Council, are asking insistently for the independence of the two Anglophone regions of our country. Because of the brutality of the police to which they are regularly subjected, the substance of their demands is not known to us to this day.

2- The Cardinal by his own life shows the way to the solution of the Anglophone problem and to a large extent the Cameroon problem. His career as a Bishop has been to head dioceses in the francophone part of Cameroon. His pastoral competence, his mastery of the two national languages, French and English, his transparent material administration in the church, has earned him high respect by the faithful. These qualities and posts neither stem from his regional origin nor are they gifts conferred to him by his British culture. Cameroon the object of his faith, Cameroon to be renewed, will be done so naturally and spontaneously without planning or calculation.

With a terminology borrowed from E. Durkheim, the Cameroon of tomorrow is like a pathological reality.The prelate refers to it as a social pathology. In insisting that we turn to God for help in this endeavour to review Cameroon and for which victory is certain, the Cardinal is not doing so as a theologian or a Catholic Dogmatist. Rather he does so as an experienced Professor of philosophy who is convinced that good sense is the best thing to be shared in the world.

Let us thank His Eminence for having made known to us his thoughts sincerely and firmly on the past the present and the future of our country. Wise men, capable old men like him are to be counted on the tip of the finger.

Professeur Pierre TITI NWEL
Membre - fondateur du
Forum des Universitaires Chrétiens
(FUC)

Introduction

It's been years that I have been thinking of what we are as a nation. Such a question is worth asking, I think, and an answer to it is worth our while. In the light of the rich teaching of the church, I have thought for quite some time on what the possible answer to the question could be. Unfortunately we have ears but cannot hear and eyes but cannot see.

This book is the expression of the love I have for my country men and women. In it I am drawing the attention of all to the danger on the way of a person that is not converted. Looking years back at the social and political life of Cameroon, one would have the impression that we are not making any progress at all. This produces in Cameroonians and especially in the youth, a sentiment of indifference and discouragement.

The consequence of such a situation is that the citizen is no longer interested in the political life of his country. Politics become for him an easy way of becoming rich, through the misuse of public funds.

Yes, our people are being deceived. But, as Hannah ARENDT says, the city, which by its nature can come to an end, depends on us to continue to be.

We may therefore ask ourselves : are we all now of the same political opinion or doctrine ? Surely not.

The much abstention and indifference shown by Cameroonians during elections simply show that they are not satisfied with their political leaders. It is the expression of a socio-political dissatisfaction of the people that should be seriously taken into consideration.

Furthermore, our elections, one after another seem to follow a set pattern. The same complaints resurface at every election : elections badly organized by the party in power. This makes the party win always at all elections and it seems to be satisfied with that irregular electoral organization. That is its life and strategy, despite its collaboration with certain political parties in the opposition.

It is very likely that Cameroon is about to begin a new phase in its political life where there will be clear ideological differences between political parties. This will help political scientists to study society with more objectivity. Thus there will be more room for true political debate. It is there alright but it is directed, not to the good of all but to that of certain individuals. What I am trying to say in this book is my own small contribution to the common good.

I am not a politician and, as a catholic priest, will never be one.

If the principles on which the life of our community is built are very much shaken, because very many Cameroonians do not take part in parliamentary and presidential elections, it is sure that our social life has to be rebuilt in one way or the other. There is no way we can avoid this. All political debate is unthinkable without the confrontation of ideas and a plurality of opinions, etc ; where Christians and believers of other religions are in the majority, this could be a very delicate situation to be in.

We may then ask ourselves, in such a situation what should the Christian do ? Any reader of this book will excuse me for the very many times I have had to cite the teaching authority of the church. This is intentional. During my pastoral work, I realize that many Christians are vey much ignorant of the social doctrine of the church. This leaves much to be desired. That is why Christians, who have no mastery of the social teaching of the church, take for pure opinion, what somebody is saying in total fidelity to that authoritative teaching, meant to educate and to inform the faithful of Christ.

I said to myself, that by citing word - for - word the teaching authority of the church, I might be helping some one some where to know what he did not know until now. The church is an old and doctrinally rich institution. She has much to teach humanity.

I owe much to many who have helped me in various ways to write this book, some helped me with their advices and criticisms; others gave me information that very much improved the quality of what I had to write; I am thankful to all those who had so well type-written what I had so badly hand-written. I have not mentioned their names, not out of ingratitude, but for obvious reasons, and to avoid any classification. Who knows, maybe while reading this book whose strength and weakness, I alone am responsible, some may find in it something completely new to them.

1

From a nation to a peaceful living-together.

1. What is a nation ?

It is a group of persons having the same origin, with the will to live together and conscious of its unity. Are we such a group of persons ? Have we the strong desire to live together as a people ? Does every Cameroonian feel at home every where he is in Cameroon ?

A nation is, as we have seen, a group of persons "made of a political community clearly delimited with a sovereign power"[1]. We can therefore say that Cameroon is a nation, a territory inhabited by a group of men and women. I am dreaming of a Cameroon that will be a "political community that finds its authentic dimension in its reference to people"[2], a Cameroon that "is and should in practice be the organic and organizing unity of a real people"[3].

I am dreaming of a Cameroon "where the people are not a shapeless multitude, an inert mass to be manipulated and exploited"[4].

---

[1] *Le Petit Robert*, Frenh Dictionary.
[2] *Compendium of the Social Doctrine of the Church* (CSDC),Liberia Editrice Vaticans,n° 385.
[3] *Ibid.*
[4] *Ibid.*

I am dreaming of a Cameroon, that is "a group of persons, each of whom - at his proper place and in his own way - is able to form its own opinion on public matters and has the freedom to express its own political sentiments and to bring them to bear positively on the common good"[5].

I am dreaming and I believe that I have the right to dream, of a Cameroon and of Cameroonians, where each citizen " is a person aware of his own responsibility and convictions"[6].

I am dreaming of a Cameroon as a nation whose citizens will be as united as the parts of a body, maintaining "an irrepressible autonomy at the level of personal existence and of the goals to be pursued".

I am dreaming of a Cameroon as a nation whose primary characteristics, like those of any good nation will be " the sharing of life and values, which are the source of communion on the spiritual and moral levels: life in society must primarily be considered something belonging to the spiritual order".[7]

Life in a society, in a political community like ours, ought to be an exchange of knowledge, in the light of the truth. "In the society men and women should be able to exercise their rights and fulfill their obligations, be inspired to seek spiritual values, mutually derive genuine pleasure from the beauty of whatever order it may be, always readily disposed to pass on to others the best of their own cultural

[5] CSDC, n°385.
[6] Ibid.
[7] Ibid.,n°386 .

heritage and eagerly strive to make their own the spiritual achievements of others"[8].

2. Public administration : the instrument of a nation

The purpose of this instrument is to serve the people, " to give aim and scope to all that has bearing on cultural expressions, economic and social institutions, political movements, laws, and all other structures by which society is outwardly established and constantly developed".[9]

Here we can truly say that a head of state is the first servant of the people he rules; members of parliament and municipal councilors are servants and not masters of those who chose them. Those elected to political positions should know that the power they exercise over the people comes from God through the citizens.

The word "minister" comes from the latin word "ministere" which simply means service or servant. It is regrettable that this meaning of the word is often forgotten.

"As an instrument of the state, public administration at any level - national, regional, community - is oriented towards the service of citizens : "Being at the service of its citizens, the state is the steward of the resources of the people, which it must administer with a view to the common good. Excessive bureaucratization is contrary to this vision and arises when institutions become complex in their

---

[5] *Ibid.*
[9] *Ibid.*

organization and pretend to manage every area at hand. In the end they lose their effectiveness as a result of an impersonal functionalism, an overgrown bureaucracy, unjust private interest and an all-too-easy and generalized disengagement from a sense of duty.[10] The role of those working in public administration is not to be conceived as impersonal or bureaucratic, but rather as an act of generous assistance to citizens, undertaken with a spirit of service[11].

3. The place of political parties in the life of a nation.

All political parties "have the task of fostering widespread participation and making public responsibility accessible to all"[12].

Political parties are called to interpret the aspirations of the civil society, orienting them towards the common good. The political parties have the duty of "offering citizens the effective possibility of contributing to the formation of political choices"[13], and they must also be "democratic in their internal structure and capable of political synthesis and planning"[14]. Today it is not democratic to govern alone. That is to say that the presence of a strong opposition in the House of Assembly is a necessity for a democratic system of government. Normally the

---

[10] *Ibid.* , n°412.
[11] *Ibid.*
[12] *Ibid.*, n°413.
[13] *Ibid.*
[14] *Ibid.*

party in power should not be afraid of the opposition in parliament.

The political parties in our country should rather fight against divisions that really weaken their political associations.

An opinion poll of any group of Cameroonians will clearly show that we belong to various political tendencies. As an observer of our political life, I have reached the conclusion that even Cameroonians of the same religious affiliation can have totally opposed political opinions, and may not vote for the same candidates nor have the same approach to the analysis of situations nor approve the same political programs.

The late Pope John Paul II said that "the church has no political system to propose" to any society.[15] The purpose of the social doctrine of the church is not to propose a third option between liberalism and the socialism of Karl MARX ; that is the work of moral theology[16] of the gospel message as a political ferment for the change of society. She does not aim at producing a political program.

The church proposes to the faithful, evangelical creativity and a Christian political pluralism. This is not an easy task. I believe that political pluralism can be brought about only by those who are involved in the life of the community, working with other citizens for the economic and social good of the people.

---

[15] Encyclinal Centésimus Annus n° 43.
[16] *Ibid.*, n°55.

Here the Christian has an important role to play. He has to live as a Christian in this world, working with others for the development of his country. He has to work for the common good, not only with those who agree with him on all he says and does, but also with those who differ with him on how a particular project should be realized. Those whose opinion may be different from ours, could have, by their contrary view, a useful contribution to make for the good of a project.

A politician who had been persecuted and put into prison before he became the Head of State of his country, had this to say : "any of us, even if he is not so important, nor has little or no authority, can change the world. This principle is logical. For, if neither I, nor you, nor him, nor all of us, do not decide to take this way, this world in which we live and have to care for it, and take part in its creation, will never change"[17].

5. The role of the civil society.

Every political community "has to serve the civil society from which it originates[18]. A "civil society is the sum of relationships and resources, cultural and associative, that are relatively independent from the political sphere and the economic sector"[19].

The raison d'être of the civil society is universal. This is so because "it concerns the common good, to

---

[17] Vadav Havel, *the Angust of Freedom*, Editions de L'Aube, Paris, 1994. P.57.
[18] CSDC- n°417.
[19] *Ibid*.

which each and every citizen has a right in due proportion"[20]. This is marked by a planning capacity that aims at fostering a freer and more just social life, in which the various groups of citizens can form associations, working to develop and express their preferences, in order to meet their fundamental needs and defend their legitimate interests"[21].

---

[20] *Ibid.*
[21] *Ibid.*

2

The political community
and the civil society.

The political community and the civil society, "although mutually connected and interdependent, are not equal in their hierarchy of ends. The political community is essentially at the service of the civil society and in the final analysis, the persons and groups of which the civil society is composed"[1].

The civil society cannot therefore be considered as "an extension or a changing component of the political community ; rather, it has priority because it is in civil society itself that the political community finds its justification"[2], the reason so to say for its existence.

It is no longer necessary to explain what we mean by the term "civil society"[3] even if it would be to avoid amalgamation and confusion with terms, expressions, and "themes which were used at one time in history"[4].

The term civil society is very widely used; "it is very frequently used in the lexicon and in a set of

---

[1] CSDC= *op. cit.* n°418.
[2] *Ibid.*
[3] The reader can easily give the content of the expression civil society by reading amongst others: Civil Society and the reduction of poverty by Sévérin Cécile Abega, clé, 1999, p.208 ; The Stade at the Civil Society in Africa:Acts of the indisciplinary colloquim, Abidjan, 1998 by Fabien Eboussi Boulaga, Issac Tamba, Alain Didier Olouga et al, nominalistic Society.The Civil Society, A Nominalistic approach, Economic Political and Juridical Prospects.The Civil Society at the Forefront at conflicts,in the Civil Society : Stake and debatee, Yaounde, Terroirs n° 004, 2005.
[4] Michel Foucault, Dit et Ecrit, vol2,Paris, Gallimard, 2001, P.574.

rules and regulations that people in a particular business or profession agree to obey"[5].

It is obvious that the civil society "is multifaceted and irregular ; it does not lack its ambiguities and contradictions. It is also the arena where different interests clash with one another, with the risk that the stronger will prevail over the weaker". That is why the state has the duty to make sure that there is "an adequate legal framework for social subjects to engage freely in their different activities and it must be ready to intervene, when necessary and with respect for the principle of subsidiarity so that the interplay between free associations and democratic life may be directed to the common good"[6].

1. The place of the minorities in a nation like Cameroon

"For every people there is in general a corresponding nation, but for various reasons national boundaries do not always coincide with ethnic boundaries"[7]. Our nation is special in this matter; it has hundreds of ethnic groups. This anthropological fact is the cause of the problem of marginalized minority peoples in our country. It is true that our country is essentially made up of minority groups. But the one and the biggest group that has much embarrassed successive governments of our country, is the English-speaking minority

---

[5] Fabien Eboussi Boulaga :The civil Society : The good use at a slogan (Terroirs, n°004, Yaoundé, 2005, P.5).
[6] CSDC, Op. cit, n° 418.
[7] *Ibid.*, n°387.

group. In fact our nation is made up of two official groups; the much bigger group which speaks the French language and the smaller group, which should enjoy "specific rights and duties"[8], speaks English.

2. The rights and duties of a minority group

A minority group has the right to be. This right may not be recognized and could even be completely wiped out by killing off a whole race of people[9]".

The church goes further to teach that the minority groups "have the right to maintain their culture, including their language; in the legitimate quest to have their rights respected, minorities may be driven to seek greater autonomy or even independence; in such delicate circumstances, dialogue and negotiation are the path for attaining peace. (Whatever the situation may be), recourse to terrorism is unjustifiable and damages the cause that is being sought"[10].

In a nation, a minority group has, not only rights, but also obligations to fulfill. Its first duty to the state "is working for the common good of the state in which it lives. In particular, a minority group has the duty to promote the freedom and dignity of each one, even if someone were to decide to adopt the culture of the majority"[11].

---

[8] *Ibid.*
[9] Pope John Paul : Message for the world day of peace, 1989, 5: A18 81.
[10] CSDC, Op. cit, n° 387.
[11] *Ibid.*

3. The English-speaking minority in Cameroon

It is evident that the English-speaking group in Cameroon "occupies a position that is inferior geographically, inferior demographically, inferior politically, inferior in resources"[12].

3.1- The consequences of the inequality between the two cultures, is that the "power to introduce a policy, to shape the course of events in things political, economic, social and cultural, lies, to all intents and purposes, entirely in the hands of the French-speaking Cameroonians"[13].

The inequality between the two official cultures is such that "at the conference table the minority political community could not speak with that dignity, that authority"[14]. of the French-speaking Cameroonians very much influenced by the strong physical presence of France. We should not forget what happened at the constitutional conference in Foumban in 1961.

France is supposed to have said there that an English-speaking Cameroonian should never become a Head of State in this country. One day I found myself face to face with M. Peter MAFANY MUSONGE in his office in Yaoundé. He was then the Prime Minister. During our discussions I asked him whether he was convinced that one day an English-speaking Cameroonian could become the President of Cameroon.

---

[12] Bernard Fonlon construct or destroy Abbia, Yaounde, Cle, 1964, P. 37.
[13] Bernard Fonlon, *Op cit*, P. 37
[14] *Ibid.*

The answer I got from him was loud and clear : dead silence.

What France, which still has a very stronghold in Cameroon wants to see happen in our country, is not the integration of the two cultures, we inherited from our colonial history but rather the assimilation of the Anglophones by the Francophones.

I will never forget the experience I had in the French embassy to the Holy See. I regret today that I cannot remember with exactitude the date, day and even the year this incident took place. While there, a civil servant of the embassy approaches me and wants to know my nationality. I told him clearly that I am a Cameroonian. Without the slightest doubt, that I could be from the English-speaking part of the country, he tells me that they, the French surely, are happy that we are succeeding in the cultural assimilation of the Anglophones.

The diplomate, discovering that I was from the English-speaking part of Cameroon, became red in the face and feeling very much uncomfortable and in doubt of what to say. He tried without success not to let me know that he was embarrassed. From that day on, I knew what was and still is the cultural policy of France in Cameroon: to make sure that the Anglo-saxon culture disappears from this country.

One can now understand why so many institutions and practices after the reunification came from the Francophone to the Anglophone part of the country. Dr Bernard FONLON makes a pertinent remark on this point : " in three years of reunification, sundry uses and institutions (...) have now come from the East into the West. In West Cameroon, they now drive on the right, the franc has replaced the sterling as legal tender, the school year has now been stream-lined to fit that of East Cameroon, and the scientific metric system has now replaced the unwieldy British measures".

"But I have searched in vain for one such use or institution brought into the East from the West. Outside its own federate frontiers, the influence of West Cameroon is practically nil"[15], on the entire national territory. Except what has recently been done forty six years after the reunification of the two Cameroon : the harmonization of the code of the penal procedure has put an end to the dichotomy between the system of the common Law which was being used in the English-speaking part of Cameroon and that used in the Francophone part of the country. The entire judiciary of the country criticized very much the existence in our country of two completely contrary judicial systems[16]. With the help of its "vast economic interests and its numerical and physical strength which is growing by leaps and bounds, and waxing stronger and stronger in Cameroon, France has the intention to assimilate the English-speaking part of the country to get rid of our anglo-saxon culture once and for all"[17].

It would seem that the political authority of the country, again very strongly influenced by France, is

---

[15] Bernard Fonlon, *Op cit*, P. 37.
[16] This opinion is largely shared by a fringe of cameroonians.
[17] Bernard Fonlon, *Op cit*, P. 37.

doing all it can to make the cultural and even the geographical unity which exist between the South-West and the North-West regions practically impracticable. The road which links the two regions is the most neglected in the republic. This is probably meant to prevent those who live in the two regions from coming often together. The road Kumba - Mamfe - Bamenda needs to be built urgently. To make myself understood, I give a simple example: to go to Bamenda from Buea, one is bound, for obvious reasons, to go through the entire littoral and the Western regions.

As far as national education is concerned, because of reunification, private confessional education has regressed and very much so. Before reunification, confessional schools had no financial problems as it is the case today. The government gave private agencies good financial aid. With the same diploma, teachers in both private and government schools had the same salaries. There was separation between Church and State. It was clear that a government school was not christian. The right of every child to be educated was respected, whether the child was in a government or private school. It would seem that in our country, there is a serious war being waged against anglo-saxon influence. Bernard FONLON underlines that "If we leave things to chance, if the will and the positive choice of our leaders do not intervene, there is hardly any hope of worthy British uses and institutions surviving and in our cultural corpus"[18].

That would be a real cultural loss to the Anglophone minority and especially to the young

---

[18] Karl Rahner and H. Vorgrimler, Petit Dictionaire.

anglophone who have no other cultural experience than the anglo-saxon. It is difficult to imagine a human being who has no culture. "Every human being is essentially a person in need of existing as a body. He also needs the world in which he lives to exist objectively and continuously ; every human being must have a culture (...) and a free self-realization for him is a must. It is by his genuine culture, the culture which is in conformity with man's nature, and with that of the world opened to the mystery and to the will of God, that man is truly natural"[19].

3.1- The Anglo-saxon minority needs protection.
The formal agreement of 1961 in Foumban foresaw neither the assimilation, nor the dilution, nor the complete disappearance of the personality of the English-speaking part of the country. It is obvious that Ahmadou AHIDJO, making use of the absolute and exceptional powers the president had, did away with his Anglophone partners in Foumban by imposing on them a gradual and political change and development which was completely different and opposed to their own political ambitions.

A political analyst decries the situation very well when he writes clearly and with precision : "what we are saying is not an original revelation, and should therefore raise neither passions nor a feeling of worry, shock nor fear. We all know and have borne it within the context of a country, that was ruled with a rod of iron. In 1972, citizens had no freedom of speech ; they had no right to vote nor the liberty to be citizens in the

---

[19] *Ibid.*

real sense of the term. The 20th of May, can therefore only have an unhappy significance. Sooner or later, to establish any political peace and institutional coherency in the country, the first thing that will have to be done, will be to correct the wrong that was done to the Anglophones. These fellow countrymen and women, whether they occupy important or unimportant places in the social and political hierarchy, make known in private, their deep sentiments of disgust, of deception and of repulsion. All of them are convinced that they are oppressed marginalized and deceived in many ways. We have no right what-so-ever to attribute to a people the results of a referendum that was organized by a bloody dictator"[20]. The daily moral torture of the Anglophone prime minister as far as some official documents are concerned, the repeated, chronic and public disrespect of the English-speaking prime minister by some ministers, worsen a situation which is already very uncomfortable. The Anglophone prime minister knows little or nothing about the study and the putting into practice of very important government policies. Where the financial situation of the country is being discoursed, the presence of the minister of finance is considered to be far more important than that of the prime minister who is said to be head of government; in financial matters, he has little or nothing to say. The minister of finance is the be all and end all in all state financial transactions. Mr Achidi ACHU and Mr MUSONGE well know

---

[20] Shanda Tonre, artcle on LE Messager n° 2133 of 24 - 05 - 2006, p.2 « Unité de quoi, par comment, et sur quelles bases ? Il est temps de crever l'abcès».

what it means in reality to be an Anglophone and prime minister in the Republic of Cameroon. "In these conditions, bilingualism, which is our national pride, becomes an artifice in the true sense of the word, a clever trick used to deceive someone. Most of the official documents are written only in the French language (...)[21].

To protect the Anglophone minority in Cameroon, we ought to have what one would call political courage, "admit their constitutive elements with the purpose of synthesizing with them in a new system that is rich, harmonious and dynamic"[22]. Those who are more powerful should therefore avoid every attempt to completely get rid of or totally absorb those who are weak. Our leaders should have the political will and courage to opt for scientific integration. Our aim is to come about a new culture which will be the combination of the good found in the francophone and in the Anglophone cultures. How should this be brought about ? " We should do three things ; the basic principles of the culture in question should undergo an examination, thorough objective and scientific examination in order to see what they are like; then follows a logical and decisive choice that is not passionate; finally, the modalities of the choice should be judiciously and energetically put into practice"[23]. To create a new culture in Cameroon, the difficulty will be that of knowing the criteria to use to get the best that is to be found in our many and varying cultures.

---

[21] Bernard Fonlon, Op cit, P. 37.
[22] *Ibid*, p.41.
[23] *Ibid*.

Doctor Bernard FONLON, that I have cited often in this book, a university lecturer very much admired by his students, tries to solve the problem : " first and in general, an element to be chosen must be true and good and beautiful in itself ; secondly it must be that which, among the three, best satisfies a specific need felt by us, a specific void in our cultural life"[24].

As a very good teacher, he points out that the new "culture to be created for the two Cameroons, if they have to be one nation, must be Cameroonian : The first principle, of which we must never lose sight, is that this culture, to be created from elements so different in their origin, must be African in its essence ; the soil from which it springs, from which it draws its nourishment, must be African ; African must be the stem into which the Franco-British borrowings should be grafted so that the sap that runs through the organism, from the root to the flower, and gives life and unity to the whole, should be African[25].

In order that the project should become a reality, "two things are absolutely necessary: firstly, African values should be studied anew, should be purified, rehabilitated and charged with new dynamism, secondly, it is of primordial importance that this African renewal and the examination and choice of the foreign elements to be grafted thereon, should be done by Africans"[26]. What should be done in practice? I cite again a long passage from Bernard FONLON. The arguments he advances here are well fitted to the subject we are talking about: "As a general rule, therefore, whenever there is question of the creation

[24] *Ibid.*
[25] *Ibid.*
[26] *Ibid.*

or the adoption and adaptation of an institution or a use of national cultural importance, no foreign intervention should be called in until African brains have exhausted themselves on the problem.

In its development, from the state of idea to that of thing, a policy normally passes through the following stages: first, someone conceives it, next it is examined, deliberated upon, elaborated, then it is adopted and finally applied.

At the stages of conception, deliberation and choice, Africans must never call for help until it is certain, beyond doubt, that the problem is above their capacity. Lack of trained personnel makes it absolutely necessary for us to rely on the stranger. Yet, except it cannot be helped, let him be called in only at the stage of application or execution ; and, even then, his work should be subject to careful superintendence.

As a rule, whenever it is necessary, at any stage, to use the foreigner's help, it must be certain that he is really a specialist in that specific field. Furthermore, and this is of supreme importance, he must be a man whose word, whose pledge, is absolutely inviolate, a man whose sincerity is transparent"[27].

In the cultural dialogue between the Francophone and the Anglophone in Cameroon "the principle of equal participation" should scrupulously be respected. It is evident that from the point of view of their surfaces, population and power, the two parts of the country are not equal, their inequality "in size, in men, in resources and in power is a self-evident fact".

[27] Bernard Fonlon, Op cit, P. 42.

"Therefore, the weakness of West Cameroon and of Anglo-Saxon influence in this federation, consequent on this multiform inferiority, is a perfectly natural outcome. It would therefore be naïve to fret against the fact. And yet, a man, as a man, does not lose his rights because he is diminutive in stature"[28]. That is why a child born today has the same fundamental human rights as an adult of fifty years old.

That is why I think that our two official cultures should be considered equal. It should be noted that "without qualitative adjective", our constitution affirms categorically that our two "official languages are English and French"[29]; that is why I agree with Doctor Bernard FONLON that for our cultural development, equal chances should be given to each of our two official cultures. Just as no man is superior to another, so too no culture is better than any other in this world.

The new Cameroon of which I dream is that which is converted, perfect and radically changed, a country ready to welcome new ways of living and doing things.

---

[28] *Ibid.*
[29] Bernard Fonlon, Op cit, P. 43.

3

The evils that are
destroying our country.

1. Bad administration

Our national wealth, that wealth which belongs to all of us, is badly administered. To call things by their name, it should be clearly said that many of those who administer our national wealth are thieves known and protected by the political or administrative authority. They steal and are free to walk the streets with impunity.

It seems to be forgotten that the State is a moral or legal person who has rights and obligations. The physical person or the citizen, what ever maybe his social or political status - head of State, minister, director of a State enterprise, civil administrator, etc. - has the moral obligation of restitution, the duty of paying back to the State what was stolen. This means that if what was stolen is not paid back, the person commits a moral fault, a sin.

To be imprisoned is not to pay back what was stolen. Even after imprisonment, the obligation of restitution still binds. What has been stolen can be paid back in money or in kind.

If one uses the money embezzled to build houses, for example, the houses become the property of the State. If the money were used carelessly, it should be paid back as soon as possible. The obligation of restitution could be inherited, could pass from parent to child.

I would add that the judiciary system which consists in arresting, locking up and condemning with severe punishment these "public predators" is already worthwhile. But the system should be looked into again.

We have heard much about the arresting of those who have embezzled public funds. But nothing is being said about the paying back to the State of the money that was stolen. Even if the money were paid into the government treasury, knowing how corruption and impunity are so deeply rooted in our administration, the money could again be embezzled by a civil servant and the chain continues.

The State could make laws obliging those who have embezzled state funds to use the money for projects of common interest for example: somebody who has stolen billions, his punishment could be to build high-ways, bridges, amphitheaters for universities, to electrify some towns, to build houses for some poor Cameroonians, etc. This would be something done for the good of the population. It is known that on the contrary, these predators, from their cells in prison, continue to direct their businesses in the society as if they were as free as any citizen.

Our forests and fauna are also very badly exploited; to continue to do this, is to violate the rights of our generations to come. Our wild and domestic animals, our forests, our plants and lifeless beings are meant for Cameroonians of today and of tomorrow. The use we make of our mineral, vegetative and animal resources, cannot be separated from the moral law.

The domination that the creator of all things allows us to have over inanimate and living beings in our country is not absolute. It is restricted, limited and conditional. The quality of the love for our neighbour is the measurement of how far we can go in our domination of beings God has put at our disposal.

We must have the good of generations to come in mind, and a religious respect of the integrity of creation[1], of that part of creation that he, from whom all things come, has entrusted to Cameroonians.

We should respect the environment where these beings live and reproduce themselves[2].

---

[1] C.E.C *Op. cit* n° 2415.

[2] According to those who want to protect the environment, the ecosystem is "the association of two composites in constant inter-action with each other ! a physico-chemical environment, where life is not possible, specific, having a spatio-temporal dimension well defined, called a determined biological milieu offering to an animal and vegetative population clearly determined relatively stable conditions of living, associated to a community where life is possible, whose characteristic is living in relationship in a vegetative place with other animals", (our translation) Fansley 193, cite par François RAMADE, dictionnaire encyclopédique de l'écologie et des sciences de l'environnement, Paris, discience, 1993, p.208.

It is evident that our forest, mineral and animal resources are very badly exploited.
What is our policy in the exploitation of our forests?
Who has to see to it that this natural wealth is well used ?
How will our generations to come benefit from the natural resources we exploit today?
Have we reserves for them anywhere?
What investments are we making for the economic future of our country?

If we do nothing today to assure ourselves of a happy future, those who have the duty to administer our resources transparently, will have to answer for their bad administration to him to whom all that is belong.

God will ask each and every one of those in charge of the administration of our common good : what did you do with the natural wealth that I gave to you for the good of my people? The Cameroonian and those who govern us should not forget the parable of the shrewd manager and the question of his master: "what is this I hear about you? Turn in a complete account of your handling of my property"[3].

Good government, about which so much is said today, goes hand in hand with the good administration of the common good. A certain number of problems are a real obstacle to the application of Laws often well thought out. There are problems linked to the management of human, material and financial resources; some are connected with human rights, with impunity, with insecurity,

---
[3] Luke 16 : 1 - 13.

and its disastrous consquencies on the development of the country.

If the Head of State or the minister administers the resources of the country with transparency, he will hear these words from the mouth of him to whom all riches belong: "well done, you good and faithful servant, you have been faithful in managing small amounts, so I will put you in charge of large amounts, come on and share my happiness"[4]. To the Head of State or to the minister who embezzles public funds, the Creator will say : "away from me to the eternal fire which had been prepared for the devil and his angels"[5]. These words are for each and every one of us who has something to do for the good of the national community. God has given to every human being he has created, something to do, however small it may be. He who uses well his gift, shall be rewarded. He who misuses his gift shall be punished.

Everyone in Cameroon is well aware that what belongs to all is badly administered. We should have the courage to say this even if it hurts some to hear it. Truth wounds but it cures and saves also. We are all in need of conversion. We are capable of administering transparently our natural resources for the good of every Cameroonian. To administer badly is not essential to man as man. None of us is born a bad administrator. Man willingly becomes a good or a bad administrator.

---

[4] Matthew 25 : 23 - 24.
[5] Matthew 25 : 26 - 41.

2. A democracy not yet sure of itself.

The foundation of democracy is the natural law which is a sharing in the eternal law, which is the plan of the government of each and every thing as it exists in the mind of God, the Creator and Sovereign master of what is and shall be. Human reason helps man to know the natural law which is found in the nature of things.

The natural law has its principles ;

(a) "As a living being, man has to respect the existence he has received from his Creator. This means that, he has to care for his life, make sure he is in good health, and above all, he should never kill himself.

(b) As a rational being, man has to behave like a person, that is to say, he has to develop his faculty of reasoning by searching for the truth always, his liberty by the mastery of his passions and his moral life by his religion.

(c) As member of the human species, man takes part in its conservation through marriage - if that is his call - by procreation and the education of children.

(d) As a social being, man has the duty to obey the authority, responsible for the organization of society for the good of all. The natural law, written in the heart of all men, enables man to know the good to do and the evil to avoid. This law must be the foundation of every democratic system, to prevent any political authority to think that he alone has the power to determine the good to be done and the evil

° Jovlivet Régis, Muel de Philosophie, Emmanuel (Vitte, Lyon - Paris, 4è éd, n° 1348, P. 293)

to be avoided. The affirmation that good must be done and evil avoided is the first principle of the natural law"[6].

Our democracy leaves much to be desired. In Cameroon, some of us believe that by talking freely about democracy, or by saying we are democratic, we become democratic. Democracy is not just a matter of words. It is expressed in the actions of those who govern the country. It is a reality. It is seen in the way the State, its basic structures, the national life and that of the political community are organized.

"An authentic democracy is not merely the result of a formal observation of a set of rules, but is the fruit of a convinced acceptance of the values that inspire democratic procedures: the dignity of every human person, the respect of human rights, commitment to the common good as the purpose and guiding criterion for political life. If there is no general consensus on these values, the deepest meaning of democracy is lost and its stability is compromised"[7].

Can we truly say that the fundamental rights of the citizen are respected in Cameroon? We cannot draw the attention of the citizen to his obligations without informing him of his rights. Duties and rights go together. Does the common good, as an end and the criterion of the regulation of political life mean anything to us? Are we a democratic country? I believe that a reply to these questions, by a Cameroonian who is able to understand and think clearly, would be negative, vague, confused or not precise.

---

[7] CSDC, Op. cit n°407.

In fact, "the Church appreciates the democratic system of government, because it is a system which enables the citizen to take part in political choices and gives him the possibility to choose and to control those who rule him, or to change them peacefully if necessary"[8].

Many will agree with me that in Cameroon, the governed have not yet the possibility to choose and to control those who govern them. For this to be possible, well organized elections is a must. Many serious Cameroonians who truly love this country begin to wonder whether it is still possible to change peacefully those we have chosen to rule us, when we think it is necessary to do so. Cameroonians are politically disappointed and disgruntled. Why are they no more interested in the political life of their country, one may ask and since when and why?

I believe that political change can take place peacefully in Cameroon as it does in some countries. Much depends on what man wants, especially on he who rules, on the political authority of the country. In Cameroon all depends on the Head of State who alone has the « supreme » power to do and to undo what he wills.

The head of man has far more to do than any other part of his body. In my opinion therefore, "true democracy is possible only in a State of law, and based on a true concept of the human person. It

---

[5] John Paul II : Encyclical Centesimus Anus 46: AAS 83 (1991) 850.

requires the fulfillment of certain conditions necessary for the promotion of the human person, through education and formation with an ideal in mind, and also through the entire development of the personality of the society, by the creation of structures of participation and of responsibility"[9].

One can again ask oneself some thought-provoking questions after a careful reading of this passage : what is a state of law ? Is Cameroon one of such states? What idea of the human person has a Cameroonian? Is Cameroon ruled in a way that all the citizens take part in the development of the country, or is the country governed for the good of a small group that usurps state authority for its personal interest?

A Cameroonian makes the following reflection : "it is indisputably true that the people of Cameroon, like many others in Africa, since 1960, were deprived of freedom of expression. All that we have been able to do in the name of democracy since 1990, was only a clever plan, a pitiable comedy which gives some the opportunity to become fraudulent politicians, those who run around the prince, and the ultimate exploiters of the coffers of the state.

They are products of agreements that are not equal and of a dishonest concept of administrative power which ends up by giving to the province of origin of the president of the Republic, a parliamentarian for less than 25 000 inhabitants as against a parliamentarian for more than 400 000 inhabitants

[9] John Paul II, Ibid.

else where; all these institutions are bound to disappear. The national assembly should be able to create for itself the conditions for her disappearance in order to finally make a place for the germ of democratic hope. Let those who had vowed never to see such or such an ethnic group govern the country not run away before the time which announces the success of all that they had abandoned.

" The speeches which caused the terrifying killings in Rwanda were like those we hear in Cameroon, the refrain according which such or such an ethnic group, because of its population density or enterprising spirit, should no more have political ambitions. Really, the resources of the complete expression of peoples, do not offer any guarantee or exclusion, nor renouncing, nor discrimination. Research has long discovered that it is neither in the name of equity, nor in the name of any equilibrium whatsover, nor in the name of any village, that those famous dishonest citizens have led peoples to war.

" History is rather rich and instructive on that accomplished art of the deceitful rulers avid of power who knew how to manipulate concepts and dogmas in order to stabilize their special advantages, thus abusing the good faith of the ordinary man. We would like them to know the truth that relations of strength are the condition for peace, and we are no more ready to tolerate these avatars of equilibrium. Democracy should be unique and integral. Let every one take his place according to his strength, let groups that are similar invite each other and work together in a circle according to their effective capacities, and their subsequent natural dispositions. The best strategy of the deceitful, which up to now has consisted in considering every action of reclaiming what someone considers his right as tribal, is no more able to resist the derogatory and embarrassing remarks about the attack organized by the same persons who exploit the State.

" It has cost the UNO much to learn that the Hutus cannot accept that the Tutsis, who are only 3% of the population should have 40% of the members of government in the name of a rickety or wobbly agreement. All this should help countries that are still not certain in the ideology of a stability which is far from being natural, pretending neither to see, nor to understand nor to be afraid"[10].

3. Is Cameroon a State of Law?

A State of Law is that which respects fundamental human rights. Every man has to live ; he therefore has "the right to develop in the mother 's womb from the moment of conception"[11]. Can we, in all honesty say that this right is respected in our country where provoked abortion, though illegal, is practiced to the knowledge even of those who should make sure that the Law is obeyed and rights respected? I doubt this. The teaching of the catholic church on abortion is quite clear :

1. " In the light of the Word of God and of reason, the church has taught always that abortion, that is to say,

---

[10] Shanda Toure : Peace is Impossible without truth in relation with forces, le Messager, n°2152, of 21 June 2006, P.2.
[11] CSDC, *Op cit...*, n°155.

the direct and deliberate massacre of an infant still in the womb of its mother is a vey serious moral fault. Human life has never been given to man as an absolute heritage, but as a treasure to be well cared for, and for which we shall one day render account to God"[12].

2. Every man has the right to develop his intelligence and his liberty through research and the knowledge of the truth. Is this right respected in our country?

3. Like every man, every Cameroonian has "the right to take part in the work that transforms our natural resources for his own good and for the good of those who are dear and near" to him. And in relation to the dignity of the human person, work to be done must have a certain spirituality and ethics. The work of man "must not be understood only in the objective and material sense, but one must keep in mind its subjective dimension, in so far as it is always the expression of the person"[13]. Work is the expression of what is taking place within the person. Because of what man is, "a society is not possible without respect for the transcendent dignity of the human person". Are those who are governing us doing all that is possible to solve the prickly problem of unemployment of our young men and women who have diplomas? "Work is essential in the life of a man. It makes it possible to establish a family, and to have the means for its subsistence. Work also helps in

---

[12] Pastoral letter of the Bishops of Cameroon on Abortion , 04/05/1979, The Social Teachings of the Catholic Church (STCC) in Cameroon p.39.
[13] CSDC, *Op cit* n° 101.

the development of a human being, for a family whose head has no employment, runs the risk of not being able to achieve all its ends"[14]. To confound the skeptics one would say that, "work is a foundation of family life, which is a natural right and some thing that man is called to. It ensures a means of subsistence and serves as a guarantee for raising children"[15]. Because of unemployment, many men no longer marry young in Cameroon. Could this not have a negative effect on our future population? It would seem that physically and intellectually it is advantageous for children to have parents who are still young.

4. Like every man, every Cameroonian has the right to found a family, to have and to bring up children, while using his sexuality in a way that is responsible. I ask myself quite a number of questions :

Can one say that the State of Cameroon respects this fundamental right of its citizens, the right to found a family, to have and to rear children?

Can we truly say that the right of every child to receive a good education is respected? I do not think so. We all know that free education is given only to children who go to public schools.

Can it be truly said that in Cameroon, parents have the right to choose for their child a school where the child can receive an integral formation, which has the final end of the child and the common good of society in view?

---

[14] John Paul II , Laborem exercers, 10 : AAS 73 (1981) 600-602.
[15] CSDC, Op cit n°294.

Can one say that our country, which is bound "to protect and to defend the liberties of the citizen, respects distributive justice by sharing public subsidies in such a way that parents would really be free to choose the school for their child"[16]? I do not think the State respects distributive justice in this area of activity, because children who go to government schools pay no fees, while those who go to schools that are not government pay fees.

Why should this garish injustice continue?

Why the discrimination between government and non-government schools?

It is undoubtedly true that if all schools were free, many parents, and maybe the majority of them, might send their children to non-government, and surely to non-government confessional schools, catholic or protestant. Many parents are convinced, and they are right, that confessional schools propose do the child values that are not found in government schools.

Our State should go very discretely and with much prudence in what concerns the State monopoly of schools, which is opposed "to the in-born rights of man, to progress, to the diffusion of culture and to choose"[17].

One would have the impression that the State wants to do away with the private schools. If not, how can we explain the injustice committed against parents who choose the private schools for the education of their children.[18]

Every Cameroonian has the right to belong to a religion of his choice, the right to "live according to

---

[16] STCC : *Op. cit.* p.138.
[17] *Ibid.* p. 139.
[18] ESSEC, *Ibid.*, p.140

the truth of his faith in accordance with the transcendent dignity of his person"[19]. For, the right to choose his religion, is "an emblematic sign of an authentic progress of man in every society"[20]. The society where these five inborn fundamental rights of man are respected is truly democratic. Are these fundamental human rights respected in Cameroon ? In my opinion, I do not think so. But we know that, man " has the primordial right to go and to come, to work, to think, to live, to found a family and to live according to the truth of his faith"[21].

4. Is Man respected in Cameroon ?

A truly democratic political system should respect Man. For this to be done, we must have a clear idea of who Man is ; he is not a spirit. Nor is he merely an animal.

A human person is a being who is conscious of himself as being the master of, and responsible for everything he does. Reason is his specific difference. If he does not reason, he becomes a mere animal. Man therefore, reasons and wills. The Christian would say that because he reasons and wills, he becomes the image of God. The Church sees in every man the living image of God.

Man " is the center and summit of creation"[22] and because he is created in the image of God, he has the dignity of a person. It is true that he is something. But he is someone, that is, something extraordinary ; he can know himself.

[19]ESEC, *Op. cit.* n°.155.
[20] *Ibid.*
[21] *Ibid.*
[22]CDSE, *Op. cit.* n°.108.

Also, "among all the creatures of the visible world, only Man is capable of God" (*Homo est Dei capax*). As a person he is created to be in relationship with God his Creator. He can only live and express himself in that relationship. His desire for God is therefore natural"[23]. He is created for God.

Man is naturally a social being. That is to say , "without his relationship with others, he can neither live nor develop his qualities"[24]. Man needs other men to be fully himself. He needs other men for inter-personal dialogue, which is vital for human existence. Man is in relationship, not only with others, but also with himself. He can reflect on himself. His spiritual interiority makes him different from other creatures : "reason, discernment between what is good and what is bad, free-will".

Man is therefore an animal that reasons, created in the image of God who wanted him to exist. He has rights and an inalienable dignity which have to be respected by every democratic society, by every society where sovereignty belongs to the citizens.

That is why the education of the child should be integral, that is to say, it should be a scientific formation which goes together with the education of his conscience. Bossuet has said: "woe betide that science which does not lead to love"[25]. And Francis Rabelais has said and rightly so that " science without conscience is the destruction of the soul". I believe that our education system does not pay attention to

[23] *Ibid., n° 109.*
[24] *Ibid., n° 110*
[25] Cité de mémoire.

60

an integral education of the conscience of the child. The education of the child without the formation of his conscience is not complete. The child must be brought up to practice human virtues which are :

Prudence or the habit which " helps reason to know in every circumstance what is truly good for us and to choose the appropriate means to attain it"[26].
Justice or the habitual disposition which " consists in the firm and constant will to give to every one what is his due"[27].
Force or the habit which " helps us to remain firm in difficult situations and constant in the search for what is good; this can help us to remain firm and constant to the point of sacrificing our lives for a just cause"[28].
Temperance or the habitual disposition which "moderates our desire for pleasures, insures the mastery of the will on instincts and makes man use material goods with moderation[29]".

5- The non-respect of the dignity of man

Is the dignity of man respected in Cameroon ? In Cameroon, how does the police officer handle the citizen who is suspected to have committed a crime? How is the prisoner treated in prison? Does he loose his human dignity as a criminal? Does he cease to be a being in the image of God who is the origin of his existence? Because the human person is what he is, he "cannot be a means for carrying out social or political projects imposed by some authority even in the name of an alleged civil community or of other persons, either in the present or in the future. It is therefore

[26]CECA, *Op. cit.* n°380.
[27]*Ibid.*, n° 381.
[28]*Ibid.*, n° 382.
[29]CECA, *Op. cit.* n°383.

61

necessary that public authorities keep careful watch so that restrictions placed on freedom or any onus placed on personal activity will never become harmful to personal dignity"[30].

The fact that a human being is " an active and responsible subject of his own growth-process, together with the community to which he belongs", his "dignity demands that he acts according to a knowing and free choice that is personally motivated and prompted from within, neither under blind internal impulse nor by mere external pressure"[31]

It is only when human dignity is recognized that the progress of all can be possible; this dignity is the same for all; it is the same for man and woman: "Male" and "Female" differentiate two individuals of equal dignity, which does not however reflect a static equality, because the specificity of female is different from the specificity of the male, and this difference in equality is enriching and indispensable for the harmony of life in the society (....). Woman is the complement of man as man is the complement of woman"[32], and this complement is physical, psychic and even ontological. It is thanks to this male and female duality that the human is fully realized. In this sense, " the woman is a 'Helper' for the man just as the man is a 'Helper' for the woman : In the encounter of the man and the woman, a unitary conception of the human person is brought about, not on the logic of self-centeredness and self affirmation, but on love and solidarity"[33].

[30]CDSE, *Op. cit.* n°133.
[31]*Ibid.*, n° 135.
[32]*Ibid.*, n° 146-147.

5-1 The handicap person

Every man, what ever his mental or physical state, should be respected. "He remains always a full human subject with rights and duties despite the limitation and sufferings affecting his body and his physical, intellectual and voluntary faculties ; he is the human person endowed with the faculties of intellectual and will ; since a person with disabilities, is a subject with all his rights, he is to be helped to participate in every dimension of the family and social life at every level accessible to his possibilities"[34].

Do we help the handicap in our family, in our society to take part in social and family life ? I do not think so. It would be seriously unworthy of man, and it would be a negation of our common humanity to admit to social life and therefore to work only with members of our society that are not handicaped, for in acting thus, we would be involving ourselves in a very serious practice of discrimination, that is to say, the discrimination of those who are strong against those who are weak and sick[35].

Do we in Cameroon willingly pay attention to the needs of handicaped citizens, to their condition of work, to the just remuneration of their work, to the possibility of their professional promotion, to the affective dimension of their lives ? The impression is given that in our country, the State has abandoned the care of the handicaped to individuals who are not even encouraged in their socio-charitable work for the marginalized in our society which claims to be modern.

---

[33]*Ibid.*
[34]CDSE, *Op. cit.* n°148.
[35]Jean-Paul II, Laborem exercens, 22: AAS 73 (1981) 634

5-2 The child is also a human person

He has rights with which he was born. These rights "must be legally protected within juridical systems". No country on earth, no political system can think of its own future otherwise than through the image of these new generations that will receive from their parents the manifold heritage of values, duties and aspirations of the nation to which they belong and of the whole human family[36]".

Many children in our country are not born in families. To be born in a family however is the first right of every child. A child who is not born in a family worthy of that name cannot be well brought up as a human person. Also, many of our children are not well fed, despite the fact that in the Central African region, our country is the richest in food variety. And we know that a child who is not well fed is intellectually and physically weak and often sick; his future is compromised for, " one of the conditions which favors his integral development is lacking"[37].

From where comes the problem of the malnutrition and of the lack of a balance diet for the Cameroonian child ? The undernourishment of our children comes from the poverty of the majority of our Cameroonian families, a poverty that I would call blamable, a poverty which is nearly a state of misery. I am saying that the poverty is blamable because our country is potentially rich in raw material and in well-formed human resources.

---

[36] CDSE, *Op. cit.* n°244.
[37] *Ibid.,* n°245.

Some years ago, a competent authority of our country said to some Bishops that some neighboring States around our country were asking for financial help. But the problem of our State was to know how they would pay back their debts ; we were then therefore, one could say, a relatively rich country ; what happen then to our reserves ? What is happening ? We produce petrol, where does the petrol revenue go or what is done with the money from petrol since 40 years of exploitation?

All every Cameroonian knows is that today, his country is one of the most assisted countries of the world, poor and indebted, without the possibility of paying its debts. Shall we one day become a developed country ? I do not despair. But the youth is despairing, we need a new generation of politicians, true patriots ; one has the impression that Cameroon is lacking ardent and patriotic citizens.

It would seem that our country is badly in need of political leaders.

What would a country become without a head ready to make sacrifices for love of his people, like that African head of State, who reduced his salary three times in order to approach the economic level of his people ? At his retirement, he had no where to lay his head. One should not therefore be astonished that the cause of his beatification has already been introduced in the Vatican by the conference of the Bishops of his country. The catholic Christian knows what I am talking about. A Swiss friend told me that the Head of State about whom I am talking - Julius

NYERERE - "the master", was the only African Head of State who had no bank account in the confederation of Switzerland.

5-3- Old men and women remain persons

Our senior citizens are also human persons who have the right to merit our attention. Their presence in our families, in our society, can be of great value. These old men and women "are an example of the link between generations"[38] and " not only do they show that there are aspects of life - human, cultural, moral and social values - which cannot be judged in terms of economic efficiency, but they can also make an effective contribution in the work-place and in leadership rules. In short it is not just a question of doing something for the older people but also of accepting them in a realistic way as partners in shared projects - at the level of thought, dialogue and performance".[39]

The old " still bring forth fruits in old age"[40], they still " constitute an important school of life, capable of transmitting values, and of fostering the growth of younger generations who thus learn to seek, not only their own good but also that of others[41]".

Our elders who are suffering and dependent on others have need of medical care and appropriate social assistance, but especially, they need to be treated with respect and love. One has the impression

[38]CDSE, *Op. cit.* n°222.
[39]*Ibid.*
[40] Psaume 92,15.
[41]CDSE, *Op. cit.* n°22

that in Cameroon our senior citizens - to borrow the American expression which expresses the respect Americans have for their old men and women - who have served their nation for years, and having just started their well merited retirement, find themselves in a material situation which is shameful to the whole country ; how is it possible that after serving the nation for so many years, some one who was paid every month during his whole career, should again be bound to prove that he was a servant of the State, that he was regularly paid by the state ? This is ridiculous. Are the archives of our ministries so badly kept ? "Lost dossiers" are easily found again when "something" is done, when "something" is given as it is said.

Many retired civil servants die without having started earning their retirement benefits! This is flagrant injustice for which the ministries concerned are personally to be blamed, and should the retired person die without having had his retirement benefits? The State will have a heavy responsibility of giving to his family what belongs to him. Let us not forget the old men and women abandoned in our towns and villages. It is necessary that the state takes measures to care for them ; that the State helps those religious women who dare, with very little means at their disposal, assure the vital minimum to these aged and abandoned Cameroonians.

The older man becomes, the more he stands in need of material care, what are the adult children doing to help their old parents? To paraphrase Ben Sirach these children should, as much as possible, help their old parents morally and materially in their loneliness and sickness. If you respect your father you can make up for your sins[42].

"The child should not make his or her parents sad during their life time. But on the contrary, if the father is becoming psychologically weak, the child should be sympathetic and care for him" Whoever abandons his parents or gives them cause for anger, may as well be cursing the lord; he is already under the lord's curse"[43].

Someone who abandons his father is like if he were insulting God. Someone who causes pains to his mother would be cursed by the Lord"[44].

In short, parents are truly the ambassadors and collaborators of God on earth. That is why," to do any harm to one's parents is to insult God, inversely God hears our prayers if we honour our parents"[45]. If you obey the law by honouring your father and making your mother happy, you will live, a long life[46].

Let every child know that obedience to God passes through the respect for and the care he has given to his parents.

5-4- The prisoner should not loose his human dignity.

What ever may be the gravity of the crime of a prisoner, he remains a human person with rights to be respected. No moral fault, what ever its nature, can

---

[42] Si 3,2-6.
[43] Sirach 3 : 12-13.
[44] Sirach 3 : 16.
[45] Sirach 3 : 5.
[46] Ex 20 : 12.

ever wipe away the image of God in man. He remains for ever the image of God. Every thing must " be done to guarantee the rights of the guilty as well as that of the innocent"[47].

Those who have the duty to establish the penal responsibility of any one must look rigorously for the truth. The procedure should be carried out with strict respect for the right and dignity of the human person.

To protect the common good, the lawful public authorithy, must exercise the rignt and the duty to inflict punishment according to the seriousness of the crimes committed[48].

Always have in mind the general juridical principle that no punishment is inflicted before the guilt is proven.

It would seem that this principle, which is essential and determinant in law, is neither recognized nor applied in Cameroon.

The punishment inflicted, which should always be proportionate to the gravity of the offence, aims at "defending public order and at guaranteeing the security of persons.
It should also be considered a means of correcting the criminal"[49].

Imprisonment should be a moral cure and reinstatement of the prisoner in the society, other wise it becomes injustice[50]. The purpose of imprisonment is to reinstate the person condemned and to promote justice that reconciles, capable of

---

[47] CSDC, *Op`cit* n° 404.
[48] *Ibid.*, n° 402.
[49] *Ibid.*, n° 403.

restoring the relations of harmonious co-existence that was broken.

"In carrying out investigations, the regulation against the use of torture, even in a case of serious crimes"[51], or any physical suffering inflicted on some one to make him reveal what he did not want to make known, should be avoided. Even in the case of a serious crime the international juridicial instruments condemn the use of torture.

It would seem that in our country torture is still used in the custodies of our law enforcement officers in order to oblige the person arrested to say something which is against his conscience, even though the Universal Declaration of Human Rights says in article 5 that: "Nobody shall be submitted to torture neither to punishment nor treatment that is cruel, inhuman and degrading".

Madame Madeleine AFITE, the well known representative in and out of our country, of the association of Christian Action for the abolition of torture [CAAT] says that torture in Cameroon takes many forms; canning, public humiliation, repugnant practices like handcuffing somebody, hanging of someone in such a way that his feet do not touch the ground, disciplinary measures in the cells....

The typical example of torture that is not so well known is that of Bernard Afush Weriwo. He died in Kumba from wounds caused by an Inspector of Police.

---

[50] *Ibid.*, n° 404.
[51] *Ibid.*

To avoid the abuses committed by our forces of law abidding officers, the delegate for Africa, of the World Organization Against Torture (W.O.A.T) advices Cameroon " to take measures and care that places of detention are visited regularly by state counsels, independent observers and associations of human rights; she hopes that these measures would reduce the practice of torture in Cameroon[52].

One thing is sure, the one who tortures humiliates himself more than the one he tortures. I believe that every act of torture is morally inadmissible and should completely be condemned. Nothing on earth should justify such an act, it humiliates the torturer and the tortured. A man is more valuable than his act. In Cameroon it would seem that recourse is made to torture motivated only by the effort to obtain significant information for the enquiry. "One could also invoke equitable justice- judgment of the one who is supposed to be guilty, should not delay, its excessive length becomes unbearable for the citizen and ends up by becoming injustice"[53].

The citizen thus unjustly treated in a state of law can take the state to court.

The majority of prisoners in our over crowded prisons are those who have not been judged:

[52] Le Messager, n° 2403 of Thursday 05/07/2007, p2.
[53] John Paul II,Speech at the Italien Congress of Magistrates (31 March 200) 4 : AAS 92 (2000) 633.x

TABLE ONE: Statistics of the population of prisoners in the ten Central Prisons of Cameroon for the year 2005.

	Bafoussam	Bamenda	Bertoua	Buéa	Douala	Ebolowa	Garoua	Maroua	N'Déré	Ydé	Tot l
Capacité d'accueil officielle.	600	500	87	250	800	200	300	350	82	1000	4 59
Effectif total	1144	435	562	321	3009	320	1211	667	494	3426	11 39
Prévenus	695	260	237		2117	170	743	270	244	2138	6 74
Condamnés	132	108	235		609	103	236	398	173	981	2 '5
Appelants	156	7	100		279	30	173	101		170	1C 6
Femmes	31	11	13	7	79	18	32	12	5		2 8
Mineurs	44	40	23	11	63	16	42	19	22	111	3 1
Personnel	98	100	50	79	200	50	70	53	58	256	10 4
Encadrement	1/12	1/5	1/12	1/4	1/15	1/7	1/18	1/13	1/9	1/13	1/11
Remplissage	191	87,0	646	128,4	376,1	160	403	191	602	343	278
Prévenus (%)	61	59,8	42,2	nd	70,4	53,1	61	40,5	49	62	nd
Mineurs (%)	3,8	9,2	4,1	3,4	2,1	5	3,5	2,8	4,5	3,2	3,4
Femmes (%)	2,7	2,5	2,3	2,2	2,6	5,6	2,6	1,8	1	nd	nd

TABLE TWO: National statistics of the population of Cameroon in 2005 the source of table one and two is the final report of - PACGED Nov 2005.

	Prisons centrales	Prisons. principales	Prisons. secondaire	Total général
Capacité d'accueil officielle	4169	9 168	2 655	15 992
Effectif total	12 400	9 354	1 351	23 105
Prévenus	7 310	3 731	418	11 459
Condamnés	3 474	4 463	792	8 729
Appelants	1 035	619	37	1 691
Cassation	32	31	-	63
Contrainte par corps	17	66	14	97
Garde à vue	141	48	-	189
Femmes	296	300	26	622
Mineurs	479	322	38	839
Condamnés à vie	58	30	01	89
Condamnés à mort	55	51	-	106
Taux de remplissage (%)	336	98	51	161
Prévenus (%)	58	40	31	43
Mineurs (%)	0,4	0,4	0,3	0,4
Femmes (%)	0,2	0,3	0,2	0,2

TABLE THREE: Statistics of the central prison of Kondegui 29 TH Dec 2009, source Germinal N° 058 of Nov 2010.

Q	C	P	Appels	Cas	Total
1	0064	0162	0029	0003	0258
2	0022	0036	0002	-	0060
3	0079	0101	0034	0001	0215
4	0011	0002	0001	-	0014
5 (Fem)	0015	0065	0007	0008	0095
6 (CM)	-	-	0012	0008	0020
7 (VIP)	-	0004	0003	0001	0008
8 (Koso)	0349	0948	0069	0002	1368
9 (Koso)	0300	1003	0074	0004	1381
10	0004	0064	0003	-	0071
11 (VIP)	0001	0003	0004	0003	0011
12 (VIP)	-	0005	0007	0004	0016
13	0025	0137	0002	-	0164
C pass	-	0047	-	-	0047
Total	0870	2577	0247	0034	3728

Le scandale de la détention préventive à la prison centrale de Kondengui, le 29 décembre 2009. *(2577 prévenus pour 3728 détenus)* Q= Quartier; C=condamnés; P=prévenus, Cas: Cassation; Fem= femme, CM= Condamnés à mort. Koso=kosovo, C. Pass = Cellule de passage

TABLE FOUR: Statistics of the population of Douala central prison of Douala for 17th August 2010

	Hommes	Femmes	Mineurs	Total
Prévenus	1571	36	27	1634
Appelants	85	3	-	88
Cassation	13	1	-	14
Condamnés à vie	5	/	-	5
Condamnés à mort	10	/	-	10
Condamnés définitifs	593	17	1	611
Gardés à vue	86	3	-	89
Gardés à vue administratif	8	-	-	8
Total	2371	60	28	2459

Source Le Messager no 365, 19th August 2010.

The data above speaks for itself, it shows that in all our prisons, the number of prisoners is far above the capacity of the prison, also from the above statistics, it is also evident that the majority of prisoners in our central prisons is made up of those who have not been judged ; this represents 58% of the prison population according to the report of the Program for the amelioration of conditions of detention and respect for human right [PACDET]- Phase 2 of the European Union.

These statistics confirm the widely spread opinion that in Cameroon detention is the Rule and Liberty the exception. This is contrary to what the penal procedure foresees and to what public authority affirms. And some inmates of our prisons have been in that state for years. The majority are young men and women and minors. Some are twelve years old! The average age in prison is thirty. Life in our prisons is very deplorable ; there, man is destroyed. I would be surprise and very much so, if our public authorities are not aware of the material plight of our brothers and sisters in prisons. On the 14th of September 2010 during a press conference, the minister of justice, Amadou Ali said that he was very much aware of the condition of life of prisoners in the Yaounde Central Prison.

In fact, making public the result of the enquiry ordered by the Head of State after the death of the journalist Cyrile Ngota in terrible conditions in the night of the 21st and 22nd 2010 in the infirmary of the Yaounde central prison, [Kondengui], the minister of justice had said that day: "The investigations made by those who direct the judiciary police and punctuated by what they saw and heard and the requisition for a post-mortem, it became clear that the police had called suddenly Ngota Ngota Cyrile and taken him to the competent judiciary authority and locked him up in the central prison at quarter 9 in the locality of 94, with a surface area of 15 meter sq which he was sharing with twenty eight other prisoners. There was space for only five beds, and the dead was spending his nights on a mattress". A simple calculation according to *Geminal*[54] makes it clear to every observer that if 29 persons occupied a space of 15sq meter it therefore means that each of them occupie a space of 0.52 sq m!

It is in such an environment that many young men and women are destroyed morally, psychologically and physically. What future have they again? The prison should be a place of correction for our youth. Do prisons favor the reinstatement of our young men and women who are in fact the product of our morally bankrupt communities? Is it true that justice is bought in our country? Is it true that the poor who takes a guilty rich man to court looses always his case ? If that were true, it would also be true, that in our prisons, there are to be found innocent persons and that outside our prisons are to be found in our towns and villages criminals in liberty. In fact it would seem that our country is a lawless state, a state without laws, a state with laws that are not observed, or a state where the economically strong is always right ; that is why in

---

[54] *Germinal* n° 065, *Reconstructing our Citizenship and Cameroon* by Jean Bosco Talla p.3.

my opinion, our country is a state where law is not respected. I do not doubt that one day Cameroon will become a state where law is respected.

LIFE AFTER IMPRISONMENT.

What is the state doing to reinstate in our national families those young men and women who come out from our prisons every year?

What opportunity of social reinstatement has someone who has lost in prison the right to means of subsistence which he had before going to prison?

What opportunity of reinstatement in the society has someone who is forbidden to take part in the life of his natural family or in the life of the village where all he owns is found? He is looked upon as being a dangerous man.

What opportunity of social reinstatement has one who, because he had been a prisoner, is always looked upon as dangerous, what possibility of reinstatement has someone who because he had been a prisoner cannot be employed by the government or take part in the political life of his country ?

What possibility has some one who after imprisonment finds himself in the same social context which made him a criminal or a delinquent, finally we can ask ourselves, what future has a former prisoner for reinstatement?

Our state and government ought to do every thing possible to enable our brothers and sisters who have spent a very important part of their lives, of their youthfulness in inadmissible prison conditions, "to adapt themselves again to a family, professional, cultural and social life"[55].

They remain our brothers and sisters of this nation.

The preparation of the prisoner for his reinstatement should begin in prison where " very often the Warder makes the prisoner undergo suffering which is out of proportion to the motive of his being in prison"[56].

This preparation can consist in improving our prison system which leaves much to be desired .The conditions in which our prisoners live are not humane. They are intolerable. They are even bestial. While in prison, conditions can be created to help the prisoner continue to practice his profession or to learn a trade. To make this possible, spacious and well built prisons are necessary. These should be built outside the towns. I have often asked myself if the New Bell Prison in Douala is where it should be. Finally, when a person leaves prison, he could be given a small capital which would help him to begin a new life in his place of origin. A prisoner should never leave the prison empty handed, if he is a young man or a young woman he or she should be helped to continue his or her intellectual or professional formation if he or she has the ability to do so .

It should be noted here that the imprisonment of someone should not be too long otherwise, it becomes dehumanising. The criminal is more than his crime

[55] *Le Messager*, n° 2403 of Thursday 05/07/2007, p.2..
[56] *Ibid*.

which is neither a fatality nor the last word of the man. What ever his culpability, man can still become better. Every criminal has, like every human being, a unique spiritual dimension which gives him the vocation to participate in a personal way in his own reinstatement in the human community. The first condition for his true reinstatement is that he should not be judged for what he was but for what he is beyond his acts, for what he is called to become . A bad man today can become a good man tomorrow, just as a good man today can become a bad man tomorrow. We should never reduce a human person to the acts he has committed. What he is, is of much value than his acts. We should always look at the criminal with the eyes of hope which make us believe that a criminal can still become a virtuous man.

5-6-THE DEATH PENALTY

The teaching of the Catholic church is clear on this point ." Given the possibilities which the state now has for effectively preventing crime by rendering one who has committed an offence incapable of doing harm, the cases in which the execution of the offender is an absolute necessity are very rare, if not practically non-existent. When non- lethal means are sufficient, authority should limit itself to such means because they better correspond to the concrete conditions of the common good, are more in conformity with the dignity of the human person, and do not remove definitively from the guilty party the possibility of reforming himself"[57].

---

[57] CECA, Op. cit., n° 469.

It is clear that in principle, the catholic Church, like many other modern and democratic states, is against the death penalty, and this out of respect for human life which is sacred even that of the murderer ." From its beginning, human life involves the creative action of God and it remains for ever in a special relationship with the creator"[58].

Why is our country still executing murderers, even though it would seem that our Head of State, Paul BIYA finds it difficult to sign a decree ordering the execution of a murderer? I understand why he hesitates to do so . He should go further and abolish the death penalty in Cameroon. Cardinal Jean- Pierre RICARD is right to ask himself -" is a state, where murderers are still condemned to death, not arrogating to itself powers that belong to God alone"[59]?

6- Is the liberty of the Cameroonian citizen respected?

To really appreciate the importance of human liberty one needs to have had the sad experience of a prisoner or to have lost one`s liberty for some time. Man is free by nature. Without his liberty, he can not be what he should be. A man is a person endowed with initiative and mastery of his acts. A free man is a being that has the power "to act or not to act, to do this or that, and so to perform deliberate actions on his own responsibility". Liberty therefore implies the possibility of choosing between good and evil, "and thus of growing in perfection or of failing and sinning"[60].

[58] *Ibid.*, n° 466.
[59] Cardinal Jean Pierre Richard in Catholic Documentation n° 2368 of 19/11/2006.
[60] CEC : Op. cit n°1732.

It is liberty that determines human acts. That is why man is responsible only for his voluntary acts. To be responsible for one's act, one must know and will what one is doing[61]. That is why, the responsibility for an act can be diminished or even gotten rid of. "The imputability and responsibility for an action can be diminished or even nullified by ignorance, inadvertence, duress, fear, habit, inordinate attachment and other psychological or social factors"[62]

The habit of doing what is good and avoiding what is bad makes man truly free. Liberty is to be found where good and justice are found. One is free in order to serve others and to respect their rights.

Man is not absolutely free to do or to say what he likes. He is not " an individual who is fully self-sufficient and whose finality is the satisfaction of his own interest in the enjoyment of earthly good"[63].

The liberty of the human being has limits, it is finite. To be free does not mean not to obey legitimate authority. "Moreover, the economic, social, political and cultural conditions that are needed for a just exercise of freedom are too often disregarded or violated. Such situations of blindness and injustice injure the moral life and involve the strong as well as the weak in the temptation to sin against charity. By deviating from the moral law, man violates his own freedom, becomes imprisoned within himself, disrupts neighborly fellowship, and rebels against divine truth"[64].

[61] *Ibid*, n°1732.
[62] *Ibid*, n° 1735.
[63] CEC, Op. cit, n° 1740.
[64] *Ibid*.

The liberty of every one of us makes us moral subjects -"Freedom makes man a moral subject. When he acts deliberately, man is, so to speak, the father of his acts. Human acts, that is, acts that are freely chosen in consequence of a judgment of conscience, can be morally evaluated. They are either good or evil"[65].

Every human being therefore has the right to exercise his liberty. For liberty "can not be separated from the dignity of the human person. Such a right should be recognized, respected and protected taking into account the common good and public order"[66].

It should be noted that: " individual liberty is exercised in relation with other human beings and every person has the natural right to be recognized as a free and responsible being. The dignity of man therefore demands of him to act according to a conscious and free choice, matured and determined by a personal conviction and not under any instinctive or external pressure"[67].

6-1- The principles of solidarity and subsidiarity: man is also free to associate himself with other men for his good or for the common good. That is why the encyclical, *Quadragesimo Anno* of Pope Pius the XIth which commemorates the 40th anniversary of the encyclical of Pope Leo the XIIIth, *Rerum Novarum*-"warns against the none respect of liberty of association and reaffirms the principles of solidarity and of collaboration, according to which the salary of the employee should be proportionate, not only to

[65] *Ibid.*
[66] *Ibid.*, n° 365.
[67] *Ibid.*, n° 135.

his personal needs but also to the needs, of his family. The state in its relationship with the private sector, should respect the principles of subsidiarity which says that a superior should not intervene where the inferior can do the work"[68].

That is" to say neither the state nor any larger society should substitute itself for the initiative and responsibility of individuals and intermediary bodies"[69].

The duty of the state and of the society at large is to help and coordinate in case of necessity, the individuals and intermediary bodies for the common good.

The state is bound to give to every citizen what is his or her due, to respect the liberty of the individual. But is that the case? " The principle of subsidiarity is opposed to all forms of collectivism, socialization of what a citizen can do and do it well. It sets limits for state intervention. It aims at harmonising the relationship between individuals and societies."

This principle "aims at harmonising the relationships between individuals and society. It turns towards the establishment of true internaltional order"[70].

6-2- The state and man: we know that man is social by nature . He therefore needs society for self fulfillment.If the state has the responsibility to give to every citizen the possibilty of realising himself " this

---

[68] *Ibid.*, n° 1883.
[69] *Ibid.*, n° 1894.
[70] *Ibid.*, n° 1885.

remains the responsibility of every individual citizen"[71]. Here we make two distinctions:

The first is that" the state has the sovereign responsibility for all that concerns the common good, it is not its place to administer the property of the individual citizen; as long as the common good is not endangered, the citizen has the inalienable right to go about his personal activities and to realize by himself the private activities that are his duty to carry out. Here the principle of subsidiarity forbids the state to interfer in the private domain"[72].

No state in the world has absolute power, whatever its military or economic strength. Every state is to serve, " to do this, it has to promote the common good to which every member of the national community has to contribute"[73].

Every citizen has to take part in the building of his nation . Never the less, the rule of the state can and should go further, " and that is where the principle of subsidiarity is at work. If because of special economic or historical circumstances (e.g a time of crises or a time of scarcity) the individual or society, finding itself in a difficult situation, can not realize their private tasks, the state should help them instead of taking over their business once and for all. It should only help the individual to come out from his difficulties"[74].

What can we say about the nationalization of private business, that is to say, about the passage of a private business to a public one? " To make a private

[71] Droguet & Ardant, New catholic Encyclopedia, Paris, Fayard, 1989, p.858.
[72] Ibid.
[73] Ibid.
[74] Ibid.

business public cannot be a general solution in economics, for this would be not to recognize the liberty and right of the individual citizen"[75].

The naturalization of private business can be for the good of all. In such a case the state should avoid directing everything with excessive and unjustified authority. When the public domain invades every thing and no longer respects the liberty of persons and their initiatives, " we have a state of providence, a state of collectivism, a central economy,and a planification that limits one`s freedom to do what one wants ; on the contrary, if the state, ignoring its mission of subsidiarity, (its mission to do what it ought to do for the common good), leaves every one to do what he or she would like to do in the context of a sort of jungle law, where the weak is crushed by the strong, and intervenes only to prevent anarchy and chaos, we have a police state"[76].

What should the state then do in this delicate interaction between the common good and the private good? The state ought " to give to the individual, maximum liberty, by promoting the best conditions for private exercise, by stimulating private initiatives in view of the common good (e g help of an unceazing planification). In a word, the role of the state is not subsidiary or accessory in relation to its specific mission; it is subsidiary only in relation to individuals and to intermediary societies which it ought to help as far as possible"[77].

---

[75] *Ibid.*, p.858.
[76] *Ibid.*
[77] *Ibid.*

4

Corruption in Cameroon

1- A systemic evil.

The word corruption has a moral connotation. It is the substantive of the verb to corrupt, which comes from latin *"corrumpere"*. Etymologically, cum-rumpere means to break what is whole. The word corruption can mean alteration or seduction; but it makes reference always to the breaking up of what is whole; co-ruptum. It is the alteration of a substance by decomposition and putrefaction. Corruption would mean abasement, decadence, deprivation, and even perversion. These meanings of corruption could be applied to someone who diverts another either from his taste or traditions or from his duties by promising him money, honor and security[1]. In general corruption is "the abuse of power for personal interest".
[2]We can say that corruption is found where there is power and laws to be transgressed.

And people are ready to sell themselves for power and money. Laws are transgressed by greedy individuals who had the responsibility to protect them.

---

[1] Eric Alt and Irène Luc : The Fight against corruption Paris, PUF, 1997, P.3.
[2] *Le Messager*, n°2403, of Thursday 05/07/2007.

According Robert Klidgaard; "corruption is to be found where an individual places in an illicite manner, his personal interest above those of the people and the ideals which he committed himself to serve. Corruption takes many forms. It goes from the insignificant to the monumentum. .It can consist in the distortion of the simplest procedures as in the abuse of the important instruments of public action- which could consist in custom tariffs or in policies concerning credit, systems of irrigation, housing, or again in the application of laws and regulations concerning public security, or in the respect of contracts or the paying back of what was borrowed. Corruption is to be found not only in the public sector but also in the private. It could exist in the two sectors at the same time"[3].

It should be underlined that the fact that our institutions or public services are systematically disfunctional, foster the practice of corruption, so much so that it becomes difficult for some one who is studying the phenomenun of corruption to make an exact difference between, on the one hand, favouratism, clientelism and generalised "piston" and the arrangements "where the other partner has to pay some money; or between interests, legitimate gratifications, and illegitimate gifts"[4].

---

[3] Robert Kligaard, *Fighting Corruption*, California, New Horizons, 1988, p.VIII.
[4] Giorgio Blundo and Jean Pierre Oliver de Sardar, *Paily Corruption in West Africa*, Africa Politics n° 83, October 2001, p.8.

One would be tempted to say that there is real link between practices of corruption and daily works of public services.

That is why, more and more, one prefers to talk about the" complexity of corruption"[5] ; a general acceptance which brings to mind" the abusive use of (illegal or illegitimate) public services by many for their private interest"[6].

Corruption is one of the evils that are destroying the very foundations of our nation. It is "destroying our social life, {...} especially our consciences. Our country is miserable because of this evil"[7].

1-1- Who is a corrupted person? A corrupted person is one who violates " duties of probity, of fidelity and of impartiality required in the exercise of a public responsibility to the detriment of a user "[8].

To be still clearer, a corrupted person is an individual who " allows himself to be bought, in order to abstain or to do his work for money or promises ; we can also talk of corruption where an individual remunerates the complaisance of a professional in order that the professional should do his work honestly or not to do it at all"[9].

If there is a corrupted person it is because there is a person who corrupts. He who offers gifts or

[5] Jean Pierre Oliver Sardar : *The Moral economy of corruption in Africa*, **Africa** Politics n° 83, October 1999, p.p. 97 - 116

[6] Giorgio Blundo and Jean Pierre Oliver de Sardar, *Ibid*, p 8.

[7] Pierre Titi Nwel, *Corruption in Cameroon*, Yaounde, Saagraph, 1999, p.9 and ff.

[8] Pierre Titi, Op. cit, p.9.

[9] *Ibid.*

presents in order to obtain for himself or a third person the doing of something, the postponement of an act or the abstaintion of doing it, corrupts[10].

According to the Bishops of Cameroon "corruption and embezzlement of property that has been confided to us, is a tragedy which concerns all of us, it is a serious sickness from which all of us are suffering and which touches all the parts of our social body. Corruption is to be found even in our Christian communities ; in our dioceses, in our parishes, in our movements and in our financial services"[11].

The Bishops are alarmed by two things concerning corruption: the first is that the example comes from above, that is to say from those who occupy important places in the administration of our society. This gives to others the pretext to do the same.

The second thing that worries the Bishops about corruption is that" our children are born and grow in this atmosphere which does not help at all in the education of their consciences making them to believe wrongly that success is not obtained by hard and honest work but by deceit and stealing"[13].

In Cameroon today, if one is not involved in the practice of corruption, if one lives honestly, one is looked upon as naïve. " Moral values do not mean much to many, in such a way that the deceitful are looked upon as courageous and intelligent. On the contrary moral rectitude, professional consciousness and assiduity at work are looked upon with disdain"[14].

---

[10] Ibid.
[11] Pastoral Letter of the Bishops of Cameroon on Corruption, n° 2.
[13] Ibid, n° 3.
[14] Ibid.

That is why the Bishops once more strongly affirm; "that corruption has reached a suicidal level in our society. It has been accepted as a normal way of life, to such a degree that many no longer have any sentiments of guilt in practicing it"[15].

What are the signs of corruption in our country? The civil servant asks, before he acts or does not act, that some thing should be done (a gesture) in his favour by the one who wants to be served. The gesture is often known and fixed before hand. It is known that for a candidate to have a place in a higher institution, he has to pay a certain some of money; a driver who has neither an insurance nor a license to drive, to go through a police check point on the road, has to give some money. It is also known that to withdraw one's money from the government treasury, the officer often would ask for a certain amount of money, or a certain percentage, etc. For a Cameroonian, corruption is also the fact that taxes paid to the tax collectors are partially paid to the treasury of the state ; the tax collector keeps for himself the entire sum collected or part of it. Every body is aware of these practices[16].

One of the very well known forms of corruption is the attribution of contracts. Instead of considering only the seriousness and the competence of the contractor who proposes his services, what is looked for is rather to know what he is ready to pay under the table. Thus as some underlined, the state is at the

---

[15] *Ibid.*
[16] Pierre Titi Nwel, *Op. cit*, p. 12.

mercy of some adventurers who are to be seen when contracts are being offered, incompetent, men and women whose one ambition is to misuse state funds. It does happens also that government officials in charge of offering these contracts ask for themselves 30 to 50% or more of the amount of money meant for the projects, as the price of their signature. By their odious demands, they slow down and some times even make it impossible to realize projects useful to the country and that foreign agencies are ready to finance. How is it possible that such persons are not punished by law?

Furthermore, according to current practice, government and private projects are over estimated. It is easy to estimate that the project needs fifty tons of cement where as in reality it needs only twenty to thirty tons, the rest is stolen by the contractor and returned to the market for his benefit.

As for the project realized with only half of the quantity of the cement that had to be used for it, it remains uncompleted or fragile and would have to be started again the following year. This situation compromises seriously the cooperation between us and friendly countries.

The state also looses huge sums of money because of the way taxes are collected. Unscrupulous civil servants are ready to cancel big sums of money owed by a contractor to the government for personal benefits. The looser is the nation, since the money which ought to have been used for the development of the country- for building roads, schools and health centers - was embezzled and misused. Encouraged by these examples, dishonest state agents also involve themselves in this illicit way of making money. Custom officers and members of the forces of law and order, extort money from the people at check points, even though they are forbidden to accept gifts when they are on duty. The license to drive is sold to inexperienced drivers or to persons who have not yet learnt to drive. In exchange for some notes, the law enforcement officers close their eyes to vehicles that are in a bad state, without lights, which cause mortal accidents to road users.

The transfer of administrative personnel or civil servants and access to post of responsibilities, are negotiated often according to a fix amount of money or on the bases of the fact of belonging to a particular group of which the civil servant in charge is at least a member.

It is also well known that teachers, professors and directors of professional and secondary schools, ask for money to admit or to promote a child who does not merit it. From the primary school to the university, recourse to money or to a gift of any kind in favour of a teacher has become a common practice. When the time for examination is getting near, school children, students and parents, disregarding every moral law, do every thing possible to get the questions before hand.

We find it necessary to say again and again that our youth is becoming more and more convinced that success is to be obtained, not so much in making efforts and looking for excellence, but in the ability to use one's power and what one has to corrupt. Of course, it is the children of the rich who are able to buy places and to give the necessary gifts to obtain certificates. But what is the real value of such certificates, since in reality those who have them have neither learnt any thing nor acquired any competence what so ever? What intellectual future, what elite are we preparing for the Cameroon of tomorrow?

Some Medical officers, nurses and matrons in government hospitals and health centers are known to ask for money to care for patients. Patients who have not got the financial means, who already have difficulties to have access to medical care because of the economic crisis the country is going through, are not able to meet these illegal demands and postpone their medical visits, a postponement that could lead to death.

Patients have thus become the prey of certain medical professionals who no longer have the spirit of sacrifice and self denial. It is a pity that access to this noble profession, which demands solid technical, scientific and moral aptitude, should be based, for many candidates, on what one has, from the time of the entrance examination to the time of coming out from the school.

Some officers of these government medical structures, go as far as stealing medicines and even samples meant for the hospitals and sell them for their own profit. The shameful trafficking of pharmaceutical products is well known. Medicines with doubtful curative effects and which therefore could be mortally dangerous are put in the market.

1-2- Our judiciary system and corruption

Corruption in the judiciary means every undue influence on the impartiality of the procedure by any actor in the system. Corruption here concerns the police, gendarme, lawyer, the prosecutor, the judge the warder and every other person who takes part in the judiciary decision. According to Transparency International, generally, corruption can be classified in two levels: interference of other powers (the Executive, Legislative, Economic , media and military) and gifts. " Political interference could be a threat, intimidation, giving money to the judges for the manipulation of nominations in the judiciary and of conditions for employment.

As far as gifts are concerned, the civil servant in the judiciary can oblige some body to give him money for work which he is bound to do ; the lawyer can ask for money to accelerate or to orient their clients to judges known for rendering favorable decisions.

On their parts the judges can accept gifts to delay or to accelerate a judiciary decision, to accept or to reject an appeal, to influence other judges or simply to take a judicial decision in favor of a client. Cases where the police falsifies proofs that justify penal pursuit are very many. It can be noticed that more and more, prosecutors do not apply the same criteria to proof presented by the police. A certain form of corruption manipulates the judicial system to take an unjust decision ; but many propose gifts to influence the direction of the judiciary procedure in view of a decision which could be just"[17].

---

[17] Le Messager, n° 2470 of 04/10/2007.

Thus according to the report of 2006 published on the 26th September 2007 of Transparency International, "the Cameroon judiciary system is the most corrupt in Africa. In the continent one person out of five interviewed who have been brought to justice admits that he had offered gifts in the context with which we are concerned"[18].

It is even said that; " 59% of persons consulted in Africa think that the judiciary system is corrupt In Cameroon, 80% of the enquiries reveal that the judiciary system is rather very corrupt"[19].

Corruption is serious in our judiciary system even though the judiciary has the mission to ensure that equity reigns. Magistrates, Judges, and Prosecutors sell their judgments to the highest bidder. Prisoners who are awaiting judgement and have no money to pay for their judgment, spend years in prisons awaiting judgment which often never takes place. This is flagrant violation of human rights and the laws of the country. And when a judiciary decision is finally taken, its execution is not evident. It is necessary that the Cameroon judiciary system have the ability to act independently from others, and some times even against the interest of the political class and of the government.

Some years ago we learnt that a judge in Spain asked and obtained the arrest of General PINOCHE who was visiting London, and that a tribunal in Spain examined the conditions for his extradition. It was a

---

[18] *Ibid.*
[19] *Ibid.*

very positive decision which however caused enormous political problems. The local action of the executive was not the same as that of the judges. I ask myself if in our country a judge would have the courage to arrest without orders from above, a dignitary of the party in power suspected of torturing a citizen or of corruption.

A judge should never allow himself to be influenced by the strategies of a political party or the private sector; he should not allow himself to be controlled by a cooperation or a group with particular interest. He always has to be impartial in taking a judicial decision. It is still to be proven that in Cameroon there are judges who are independent and impartial and that the Cameroon government would like us to have such judges.

Our courts have become, for the poor who are to be judged and who have nobody to intervene for them, places that frighten them more and more. They find themselves exposed to injustices of every kind. The situation is particularly painful for those who are accused innocently.

Public contracts are occasions for asking for more than what is required and this at the cost of the tax payer. The offering of public contracts is disorderly carried out. Every one knows that in the offering of these contracts by government agents, all is done as if we were dealing with a family or a tribal business.

There are very few Cameroonians today who believe in their judiciary system. But it is necessary to have confidence in it for when this is lost, popular or mob justice takes its place. Thus, one of the evident consequences of corruption in our country is mob justice. It is the expression of the abuse of confidence of which some Cameroonians are victims when arrested by the police or the gendarmes.

Cameroonians often complain that thieves caught and taken to the police are soon found going round the town freely and threatening the lives of those who took them to the police. That is why, without any respect for human life, Cameroonians think that the best solution to the problem is mob justice, that is killing the thief.

1-3- The evil that corruption is doing in the judiciary is done to the country.

According to Charles NGUINI, a lawyer and president in Cameroon of Transparency International, "corruption weakens justice, by refusing the victims and the accused the fundamental right to a just and impartial judiciary procedure.{…} A corrupt magistracy divides the community; a judiciary system that has lost its value because of gifts to the judges, undermines the confidence a citizen should have in the public administration of his country; when corruption is accepted beginning with the one at the head, the judiciary system loses its value and undermines the confidence the citizen should have in the administration of public affairs"[20].

Concerning corruption in our economic life, Davide Koshel who is in charge of programs for

[20] Le Messager, n° 2470 of 04/10/2007.

Africa and the Middle East at Transparency International in Berlin has this to say: "one observes a correlation between the level of corruption in the judiciary and the level of economic progress, given that the certainty of the execution of the contract or the payment of the contractors is very important for the investors and constitute the conditions of the development and of the progress"[21].

"Corruption weighs heavily on the working of justice and the economy and is a serious handicap for the harmonious working of society"[22].

Thus in Cameroon corruption destroys completely the value of justice and those who try to apply it . Justice becomes diluted, partial, and unjust. Judgments rendered are no longer for equal crimes. They are false because of impartiality. Consequently, some juridical scientists have observed that corruption slows down the progress of the law . Also, "a corrupted judge gives orders of incarceration which are inconsequential with the crimes, and this gives the wrong interpretation of the legal texts which prevents the progress of the signs of law"[23].

Because Cameroonians have lost confidence in their legal system, they use "other means to obtain justice for themselves such as what is called popular justice: summary execution by lynching a thief, the revenge between individuals in conflict"[24].

---

[21] Le Messager, n° 2470 of 04/10/2007.
[22] Pierre Titi Nwel, *Op. cit*, p. 67.
[23] *Ibid*.
[24] *Ibid*.

Because of this social evil," honest judges are in fact ostrasized and marginalized by the corrupted system: thus society loses its competent and integral judges. A judge who is influenced by the amount of money given to him by the one to be judged, loses his independence and judicial conscience. And when this happens, juridical insecurity installs itself gradually but surely in the society"[25].

Corruption destroys the economy of the country. An authoritative voice, the voice of Mr Sally DAIROU, a former Minister of Public Service and Administrative reforms says : " Corruption makes the state to suffer heavy economic losses. Contracts concluded with Cameroonians or with foreigners, involve always envelopes which are given to government officials who have to pay the contractors and control the projects. The sums of money paid to government officials are obviously included in the cost of the project. Thus a project which would normally cost only 1 billion, in the end really costs 2 billion or more"[26].

"Corruption is a factor which reduces drastically national revenue, makes it impossible for the state to fulfill its social obligations which are: the building of schools, the building of health centers and the building of roads"[27].

One can say that corruption is " the violation of human rights, in as much as it prevents the population from enjoying the fruits of progress and

[25] Pierre Titi Nwel, *Op. cit*, p. 67.
[26] Cameroon Tribune of 09/04/1998, cited by Pierre Titi Nwel, Op. cit, p. 68.
[27] *Ibid, p.72.*

becomes a permanent negation of the right to development"[28].

This social evil increases the cost of transactions and incertitude. It leads generally to inefficient economic results, and in the long run it becomes prejudicial to exterior and interior investments.

This system leads to a bad distribution of talents for research.

It leads business houses into a sort of underground economy, "which lessens the resources of the state in such a way that more and more heavy taxes are paid by less and less tax payers"[29].

Corruption " imposes regressive tax which weighs heavily on commercial activities and on the services of small business houses. Corruption causes much damage to the legitimacy of the state"[30]. It kills the state economically. It makes " the building of a solid nation founded on what the individual citizen can do difficult. Individuals are born equal in a society where social functions are differentiated and complementary, and where the society gives to each of its members by means of structures of formation, with equal access to important position by means of personal efforts"[31].

On the contrary," this social evil takes the place of personal efforts: it makes a mockery of the social principle of equality of chances and also of the role given to the structure of formation as such"[32].

---

[28] *Ibid, p.72.*
[29] Pierre Titi Nwel, *Op. cit*, p. 67.
[30] *Ibid.*
[31] *Ibid.*
[32] *Ibid.*

Corruption " attaches little or no importance to the fundamental capital which is the personality of the individual consolidated and enriched by formation, and which gives to every citizen access to every post and leaves to chance the possibility of the necessary adaptations"[33], as he goes on in life, for the harmonious working of social life.

Schools are being degraded by corruption. "Children who have the thirst for effort lose it. Children adopt for models of life, the practice of intrigues and for ways to success, dishonesty and the corruption of teachers. A teacher who, as a school child corrupted his teachers to allow him to go from the lower to the higher class, finds the solicitation of his school children normal. Our schools are therefore producing for our society incompetent citizens who are not able to take part in international intellectual competition of the 3rd millennium"[34].

What future has a country whose citizens are not competent? Such a country would never be independent, it would remain a school child of its neighbors. It would never attain a respectable social and economic level of development. Corruption deprives the state of its power to rule. It is the state that makes sure that rules and regulations that regulate life in society are applied equally to every body. It is the state that creates a republic and citizenship. It is the responsibility of the state to instill in every individual the sentiment of being a citizen like every other member of the social community.

---

[33] *Ibid*.
[34] *Ibid*, p.73.

This sentiment which consists in the desire to live together is still embryonic in our country. Once more we say that corruption is an assassination of the country. It is high time the government were aware of this trick .

Corruption encourages impunity, one of the crimes against a nation which" has a collective desire to live together, where solidarity between the members is not a phenomenon to be left to the wimps and caprices of the individual or to ways of his behaviour. Solidarity requires that a member of the community should do or not do certain things"[35].

" But because of generalized corruption and its effects, Cameroonians no longer agree on what can unite them as a people : access to power, the exploitation and the equitable sharing of the country's riches, the education of the youth.

There is a sort of cacophony amongst Cameroonians on the electoral code, the organization of elections, the influence of foreign companies on the economy of the nation, the obligation for all to work for the common good, love for work well done or the passion for what is easy to do and of intrigues with the young"[36]. All this shows that we have no national conscience. And if we have no national conscience, it is because it has been stifled by impunity which profits those who corrupt and the corrupted. They are many and we know all of them.

---

[35] *Ibid*, p.74.
[36] *Ibid*, p.75.

1-4- Sexual corruption of children.

When we talk of corruption in Cameroon, we do not think of that other type of corruption which can completely destroy a nation. It is the sexual corruption of children in our society. Today one is astonished to hear what is said about the Cameroonian child: It is a child who is a martyr : it is a child sexually abused by adults: it is a child who endures sexual violence: it is that child-citizen of tomorrow destroyed psychologically for life. This situation is grievous. It is necessary, not only to denounce and condemn it energetically, but to act and to act immediately to correct the situation. Civil, political, judicial and moral authorities, should do all that is possible to prevent the elimination of children which is a radical destruction of the nation. The effects of this evil are multiple. Sexual abuse of little boys and girls is a shame to our society. It is scandalous.

Empires, civilizations and individuals have been destroyed by this form of immorality.

How do we explain the progress of the raping of children in our society? One of the causes of the continual presence of this evil in our society is promiscuity. The mirage of the town makes more and more young men and women leave their villages for the urban areas.

Parents send their children to towns with the conviction that: "they will learn to defend themselves", but in towns there is no habitation for every body. There is no work for every body. They pile up on one another. Parents go out in the morning to see what they can do to provide at least a meal for the family for the day and the children are left to fend for themselves. Since they are hungry, they end up giving their bodies to lawless adults who have no faith. What these adults give them may be just sweets, a locally made cup of yoghourt and other things that children madly love. Some shameless parents encourage their very young daughters to practice prostitution.

From some terrible stories told by children who have had this experience, it is said that those who rape them say that what they are doing with them is just a play. The children say that they use on them lubricants like vaseline and other products that they do not know, small spoons and forks. These practices, are purely and simply diabolical, satanic. After raping them they are given strict instructions: they are told never to let anybody know what happened. If they reveal it to anyone their parents would become mad or will die. These are all lies! But these little ones believe in them.

These abuses of little children are also caused by the poor living standard of their parents: the children of these poor parents who can barely manage with very little money or food or who eke out a miserable existence in cardboard shacks, and are often away from home all day and some times all night are like preys for these lions roaming around looking for their preys. A child who is thus abandoned by the parents is constantly in danger of being abused.

Even children whose parents are rich do not escape the evil of moral corruption of little boys and girls. By the fact that they are often together with children whose parents are poor they end up by imitating them. What is to be said of those rich parents who, realizing that their child has been raped, prefer not to say anything about it in order not to soil the reputation of the family? Often children between the ages of 6 to 10 years, victims of rape, and whose parents had the courage to speak about it publicly, all the little girls were no longer virgins.

What should be safe guarded? The reputation of the so called "good" family, or the psychological balance of poor and innocent children, whose parents become accomplices of such an atrocious evil just because they lack the courage to expose the evil doer?

Finally one of the causes of moral corruption of children is the resignation of parents as far as the sexual education of their children is concerned. The mother does not talk to the daughter about the sexual life of a woman neither does the father to the son about the sexual life of a man. And so all ends there.

Every time a child asks a question concerning sexual life, the right answer adapted to his age should be given. What he should be told today should not be postponed for tomorrow ; often the child has already some idea of the answer to his question; it is therefore necessary to talk to him about it. As long as parents leave to the television, to newspapers and to films the responsibility of giving answers to the questions that their children ask them about their sexual life, the great danger would remain. They will leave their children to be influenced by the pervasive audio visual programmes. What can be said about films and televisions which do not make it easy for the family and the society to lead a harmonious life? Parents are and will always be models for their children.

Often we forget that a child of today looks for a model to imitate. The child of our time looks for his model on the screen of the television or film. Without the help of the parents, the child is like a sheep that just consumes any thing. He swallows any thing he sees on the screen. The little girl wants to verify what other girls a bit older than herself say or what a star does in a film. Gradually she becomes interested in the stories and what the stars do on the screen.

A girl of twelve once said that her mother knows nothing about sexuality because the only reply she had for her when ever she asked her a question about her sexual life was: " I am tired". She therefore went to the other girls to look for an answer to her question, their reply was, go to the internet."I therefore conceived and aborted she said, with the help of my girl friends". If parents do not give themselves enough time to bath their daughter when they are young, how would they know that their children had been victims of sexual violence?

The series of rapes that we deplore and condemn today do not take place necessarily in rooms in hotels by those who rape children {pedophile}. It is sad to say that these immoral acts also take place in the homes of these children. Retired adults or neighbors who have nothing to do and men who would least be suspected abuse the children of their neighbors who dare say nothing because they have been threatened or corrupted.

A Little girl once recounted how the mother of a young man who was raping her knocked on the door of the room where she was being abused, pled to her son saying: "leave her to go she has cried enough". Then she said to the little girl: "Next time don't come here again".

In some night clubs in Douala, little girls are practically sold to adults one would least suspect to be so sadistic. Little girls of nine to ten years old are taken to rooms prepared for these immoral acts behind the night clubs where they are abused by these adults.

When my collaborators were carrying out an enquiry on this matter as a result of complaint by some women in Douala, it was discovered that some so called men of responsibility in our society are involved in the practice of this evil. During the enquiry my collaborators asked a police man to undertake an official enquiry to put an end to this evil practice in a night club ; he declined and said : "Fathers, you want me to arrest my Boss"?

One day the mother discovered that there was a terrible odour coming from the body of her daughter; the mother looked at the child and the child said "mama I have done nothing". Doubting what the daughter claimed she took her to the hospital to be sure. To her surprise the doctor would not give her the medical report she wanted but prescribed antibiotics advising the mother to be more vigilant over her daughter. But one day she discovered fresh sperms on the underwear of her daughter. This time the medical officer told her the daughter had lost her hymen or she was no longer a virgin. With this medical report, she went to the police so that the one who raped her daughter might be arrested. The parents of the boy went immediately into action. They started negotiating with the parents of the girl, then with the police who made the enquiry so that the boy who was still with the police might not be brought to trial. It is to be understood that the rapist was still considered innocent ; never the less, the commissioner of police was asking for a sum of one million francs for him to be released. If the family of the boy who raped the girl did not bring that sum of money, the rapist would be brought to court. All ended up with the boy being released because the mother of the girl refused money that was being given her to withdraw her complaint and, the mother of the boy who raped the girl gave the 1 million frs to the commissioner. Children who come from these places where they are raped speak of the inhuman torture that cannot be described.

Causes of continuous rapping of children in our society.

I think that the school is no longer doing its work in the fight against this evil. It has even become for the adolescent a place where sexual trade goes on.

One hears about "STN" which means sexually transmitted notes[37].

In a quarter in Douala, a teacher who is known to be a rapist of children, said to one of his victims that: if she dared to tell her mother about the adventure, the mother would die. With the help of " justice and peace" commission of the Archdiocese of Douala, this rapist is in the New Bell prison since the month of June 2006.

Who has never heard the story of little girls who fight before their teachers because of love affairs. Some of them run away from school because of their shameful behavior.

If the school no longer protects the child, it is because parents no longer do their work. There are families where immoral acts of incest abound with impunity. The causes of this practice differ from one family to the other. One of the causes is promiscuity; in some families boys and girls sleep on the same bed. A young girl once told me that she wanted to abort because the child she was carrying was the child of her senior brother!

What is more difficult to describe and to bear for children in this escalation of moral and psychological misery, is when a father has sexual relations with his own daughter or daughters. Two things may happen either the mother knows what is happening and

---

[37] We read with a lot of interest the recent work of Jean Emmanuel on sexual harassment and deontology in the university milieu,Yaounde, clé, 2011, in which the author breaks the silence on odious practices in the university milieu, and rebounds on the school milieu, where by victims are most of the time young students.

keeps quiet in order not to lose her husband or pretends to know nothing about what is happening because her children are under serious threat from their father. Some times a mother knows for certain what is happening but is afraid to talk about it for fear that her husband will stop giving her food money. In certain situations, courageous women have abandoned their conjugal homes having known and denounced what their husbands have done with their daughter. But they leave their children with their psychologically unbalanced father. Such is the case of that young girl of 17 years old, a school child in a government collage, who revealed to the diocesan commission of justice and peace the incestuous life she was leading with her father ; before she did so, the commission had to swear that, this would not be brought to court. Without this oath she was not ready to speak, for fear of reprisals. Her mother had abandoned the family when the girl was ten and her junior sister three years old. Their father and the two girls were living in a three room house where each person had his or her room but her father abused her and her little sister who was now ten years old. They wanted to go and stay with their mother who was now suffering from depression, but she refused because she had no means to bring them up and to nourish them. What was to be done? Were the two girls condemned to accept their father's sexual madness?

The catechism of the catholic church teaches" that rape is the forceful violation of the sexual intimacy of a person. It does injury to justice and charity. Rape deeply wounds the right of the victim to respect, freedom, physical and moral intergrity. Graver still is the rape of children by parents or those responsible for the education of the children entrusted to them."[38]

What do we say about the shameful practice of buying and selling of our children coming from the rural areas ? They are boys and girls whose ages vary from six to nine years. Some fairly rich families look for these children from poor families as house servants on a salary of 5000 frs per month. This salary is paid, either to the parents of the child in the village, through the person who looked for the servant, or through the guide on the spot to be given to the child later on. The situations that we know have all shown that there is no single example where the salary accumulated was paid to the child. The child is fed and may never have his salary.

What is the nature of the work done by these children? The families that employ them do not want to employ house servants that cost much and who have to be declared to the social insurance . The little child without any body to defend his or her rights, does every thing. In the morning she is the first to rise up, she empties the dust bin, washes the car or cars, goes to look for bread for the other children for break-fast, sets the table and prepares the children for going to school. Once every body leaves the house, she has to clean up the house, wash clothes, iron them and prepare the mid day meals. The child - servant, because of this hard work, becomes old before his or her adulthood. The child - servant is a child who had

---

[38] C.E.C.A (catechism of the Catholic Church), *Op. cit*, n° 2356.

been sacrificed, he is the last to go to bed. And he spends his night either in the kitchen, in the laundry, or in the store or in the garage. When an object is missing in the house, he is the thief who is beaten and humiliated. Some times the girl servant is sexually abused by the young men in the house or/and the head of the family. The girl servant finally is obliged to leave the house for the street where she is finally involved in child delinquency. The family that welcomes her as a servant, complains to the person who brought her from the village and asks him or her for another victim...

Another shameful practice is that where mothers advice their daughters to become prostitutes. They find nothing better to say than these words which they should be ashamed to pronounce: " I thank God who gave me a daughter to help me to bring up her followers as does the daughter of my neighbor". One day a young girl of fourteen complained about her mother. She was expecting a child and her mother advised her to abort in order to continue her life as a prostitute. When the mother was asked why she was encouraging her daughter to be a professional prostitute she replied, looking serious, that she had a big project for her ; she was preparing her to become a prostitute in Switzerland. Also her daughter should not conceive and worst still put to birth. That is why the abortion had to be provoked at all cost.

With such diabolical practices, how can abortion and sexually transmitted diseases be wiped away from Cameroon?

In hospitals nurses say that they are aware of the fact that provoked abortions are undertaken with the complicity of the mother.

I have spent quite some time on these abuses but we know only the visible part, the tip of the iceberg. The evil is profound and there is still more about it that we do not know. Children who had the courage to make known what happened to them, are intimately destroyed by their neighbors, teachers, their parents, and certain persons who would least be suspected, who are the real criminals. What can one do when it is the children themselves who do not want any thing to be done to their parents, when it is the children themselves who protect their parents for fear they would be alone? In your opinion what is the future of these children? It is an unhappy future, a future destroyed forever. We are not being fatalistic.

What should be done to pass from a child sacrificed to a child sanctified? Parents who abuse their children must themselves have been, some time in their childhood, victims of these abuses. If they have not acquired a spiritual and human maturity, they remain forever children and can only reproduce in their own children what they underwent themselves.

What future are we preparing for our children ? What teachers do we want for our children? They have been very much wounded and these wounds would be very difficult or impossible to heal. One can go as far as affirming categorically that these wounds are irreversible. Those who govern our society have the serious responsibility of making sure that these young ones are protected. They should make sure that the laws protecting the minor are put into practice. Priests and those who have the responsibility of educating these children have the duty to use all means to denounce the evil of child corruption when ever necessary in order to protect these children who have no body to defend them.

Many of these children are frustrated and ask themselves where to go and to whom to go? We should learn to be welcoming to them. We should not judge them but rather listen to them attentively when they have the courage to come to us. Our country already ratified since 1990 the convention which protects the rights of children all over the world, but in practice what is happening is that those who should protect these children are the ones who violatc their rights. Some parents say: "he rapes my daughter every day" ! And have the courage to add : "what do you want me to do"? It is necessary to denounce and to talk about it.

We should love our children and be proud to leave them a country where order and respect for the body of the other, especially the bodies of little children reign. We love these children when we denounce those who by sexual violence violate their innocence and profit from their vulnerability. We love these children whenever we ask God to give them parents, those who watch over them, educators worthy of the name so that what is happening today may not happen again tomorrow.

We strongly wish " that the civil authority should seek to create an environment conducive to the practice of chastity. It should also enact suitable legislation to prevent the spread of grave offences against chastity, in order to protect minors and those who are the weaker members of society."[39] The state has the bounden duty to promote the respect and the dignity of the human person.

2- The causes of corruption.

We have seen corruption in all its forms: in the awarding of contracts, in the world of colleges and universities, in our judicial system, in the economic life of the country, in our ethical life. etc We have also seen the influence on our national life: a Cameroonian child is born and grows in an environment of corruption; moral values are treated with contempt ; ethical rectitude, professional consciousness and assiduity at work are not taken seriously", corruption is accepted as a way of life! What then are the causes of corruption?

Let us first look at the meaning of the cause of a thing ; it is that from which a thing takes its origin. There are four types of causes: the formal cause- "What makes a thing to be what it is"; the efficient cause - "what produces an effect" ; the final cause the reason for making a thing: the material cause-" that from which something is made". It is evident therefore that corruption being an effect, its causes are therefore efficient and many.

2-1- Money

The principal cause of corruption is cupidity or a very strong desire for money. "Cupidity favours a situation where every one thinks only of himself,

[39] C.E.C.A, *Op. cit*, n° 494.

where the poor are crushed ; in such a social environment, people look for positions of responsibility to buy, not to serve, but for personal financial advantages. For, the love of money is linked to the love of power which gives easy access to money." Nothing is more dangerous than the immoderate love of money[40].

That is why an immoderate lover of money is never satisfied[41]. We should never put money above every other value[42]. Money is a good servant but never a good master[43]. And even as a good servant one has to be careful with it because it corrupts.

The love of money hardens the heart of man, makes the rich insensible to the problems of others, and is the cause of injustices whose victims are always the poor. It is true that among us there are men and women who are rich and honest. But it is difficult but not impossible to become very rich and honest. We should not serve money. Rather money should serve us.

Money is not bad in itself. It is even good if it is shared with those who are in need. It is bad if man uses it only for himself, to satisfy his passion and to dominate others. Money is deceptive, because at death, it looses its value for the one who had it. The psalmist was well inspired while meditating on life: " we humans are like grass or flowers that quickly bloom but the crushing wind blows and they quickly

---

[40] Pastoral letter of the Bishops of Cameroon on Corruption, n° 31.
[41] Sirach 10 : 10.
[42] Ecc 5 : 9.
[43] Tobit 5 : 19.

wither to be forever forgotten"[44]. Our world today has two masters: God and money. But only one of them is the true master: God ; money is not a true master and it is not a true " God". Money attaches us to this world. The true master leads us to heaven, a good that last for ever. We should be free in the use of money and generous to the poor. We should not be slaves of money.

2-2- Misery

One of the causes of corruption is the misery that is caused by the economic crisis we are going through, an evil which continues to make many suffer: "some citizens are tempted to believe (and wrongly so) that corruption is the only possibility left to them to better their condition of life"[45].

2-3- Political, ethnic and family interest

These interests "blind us and prevent us from fighting against corruption"[46]. We have the tendency to excuse and to cover up the faults of those who are near to us by political, family or tribal links ; in doing so, we favor impunity which is a serious obstacle.

2-4- The purchasing power

The diminution of the purchasing power of the civil servant, is one of the causes of corruption. In this situation government services are sold to the client who bids highest.

---

[44] Psalms 102 : 15 - 16 .
[45] Pastoral letter of the Bishops of Cameroon on Corruption, n° 32.
[46] Ibid .

2-5- The lack of equipment in government offices

It would seem that : " In the judiciary the lack of equipment and personnel are the causes of corruption. The working conditions are out- of -date: with old typewriters, with neither computer machines nor electric typewriters, the employee works without any smile in a dirty environment, surrounded by dusty dossiers, without any cupboard to arrange them. That is the source of the difficulty of writing the many decisions taken in court. Confronted with this big demand, and with the thousands of dossiers before him to be studied, the court clerk is tempted to sell his services to the highest bidder waiting to be judged. Further more, the workers are fewer and each of them is expected to do the amount of work his physical fitness does not allow. Thus the selling of services in the judiciary, and the victims are those awaiting judgment"[47]

2-6- The causes of corruption at the customs.

Here the causes are many and sundry:

a- "The very slow treatment of dossiers at the customs, is similar to the slow administrative handling of dossiers in Cameroon. In introducing many ways of paying custom duties on imported goods or in delaying as long as possible the getting out of these goods from the ports, the custom officer causes tension or disorder in the activity of the importer, forcing him to negotiate"[48].

b- The custom fiscal system concerning the rules and regulations governing the importation and the

---

[47] Pierre Titi Nwel, *Op. cit*, p. 54.
[48] *Ibid*.

exportation of goods: "for certain goods like computers and vehicles, custom duty is still very high....". Custom duty, on the computer, an instrument very necessary in business administration, and the automobile, is respectively 40 and 50%.

Such high taxes naturally lead to fraud, bargaining and corruption"[49].

These are some causes of corruption: "The immoderate desire for money, low salaries, misery caused by the economic crises, bad conditions of work, impunity and ethnic family and political personal interest. We could ask ourselves the following questions: why are our laws not used to bring to trial the corrupted and those who corrupt? Do poverty and the bad conditions of work justify the practice of corruption"[50]? The answers to these questions are surely negative.

3- The fight against corruption

What should be done to wipe out corruption in Cameroon? One is tempted to say that it is impossible to imagine a Cameroon without he who corrupts and the corrupted. In my opinion it is possible to completely get rid of corruption from Cameroon. Corruption is a moral evil which concerns man created with the faculties of intellect and will. He can therefore be converted. He is able to decide to do what is good and to avoid evil all his life. We can efficaciously fight against corruption if our country is a state where individual rights are respected, where

---

[49] Pierre Titi Nwell, *Op. cit.*, p. 55.
[50] *Ibid*, p. 56.

nobody is above the law and where those who govern have the necessary political will. The empire of impunity in Cameroon is the reservoir where he who corrupts and the corrupted do what they like.

The Bishops proposed to their faithful and to all men of good will "To oppose corruption in all its forms and tenses {...}, to take together the decisions to wipe away from our ways of behaviour, all corruption , in the church, our public and private places of work and every where it shows itself"[51].
If all believers in God want corruption to disappear from Cameroon, it would disappear. It would seem that in Cameroon the majority of those who corrupt and those who are corrupted are believers, that is to say, are Moslems and Christians! What have they done with their faith? Faith without good works is dead .

For a Catholic in Cameroon, the real cure against the immoderate love for money is sharing. " The goods of the earth are not for egoistic and personal profit. They are meant to be shared for the good of all. All that we have was given to us by God for our good, for the good of those around us, for our families, for the poor and for those who are sick and in need of our help"[52].
The Bishops also say : "The remedy against poverty is work well done. "Every body knows that our country is rich, rich in natural resources of every kind, rich because it has citizens who are competent and well formed. We ought to have been years ago a

---

[51] *Ibid*, p. 34.
[52] Pastoral letter of the Bishops of Cameroon on Corruption, n° 35.

very prosperous country without the problem of unemployment. Because of corruption, embezzlement and bad administration of what we have, we ourselves are the first to be responsible for the under development of our country"[53].

The remedy to sordid interest is good government says the Bishops. "Clarity in keeping accounts, the decision of those in authority to work, not for themselves, nor for their tribal and political interests but for the country, for the common good, for the true happiness of all"[54]. Finally the Bishops proclaim that: "Not to speak clearly about corruption, would be culpable silence. Not to fight against it energetically, would be inacceptable neutrality. And not to do any thing against it, is to betray our people."[55] Every body should have a good knowledge of this evil in order to cure it ; Cameroonians everywhere should be conscious of the rights and duties of every citizen, in order to be able to denounce corruption and fight against its effects everywhere in the country, especially among the youth who are looking for good examples to imitate for their harmonious up bringing. All of us have the duty to fight against corruption in all its forms and to restore peace and justice in our country.

Enquiries made by Gerddes - Cameroon proposed some remedies against corruption: " drawing up of appropriate laws and ensuring their effective implementation, taking off dissuasive and punitive measures against the offenders, more determined and

---

[53] *Ibid.*
[54] *Ibid.*, n° 37.
[55] *Ibid.*

sincere involvement of the highest authority of the state in the fight against corruption (example comes from above), having enough senior staff and improving the working conditions of all the workers, simplifying the procedures at the customs and the education of citizens on their rights and duties"[56].

To these remedies can be added article 66 of the constitution and the dispositions of law no 003- 2006 of 25 April 2006 which talks about the declaration of goods, the UNO convention against corruption ratified by Cameroon (CF annex 3) and the convention of the UNO against organized international crime. Transparency International is of the opinion that corruption in the judiciary can however be remedied. That is why in this report this organization proposes a remedy which is the reform of the judicial system. Leonard Ambassa, a Lecturer in the Catholic University of Central Africa (CUCA), is of the opinion that one of the possible remedies of corruption in the judiciary would be "the mobilization of magistrates, the culture of good results among them and the popular education of the people in judiciary procedure"[57].

Enquiries show that, for a Cameroonian, there is a very close link between corruption and political system, "and every action which is in favour of the democratization of the political structures of the country, should take part in the fight against corruption"[58].

---

[56] Pierre Titi Nwel, *Op. cit*, p. 77.
[57] Le Messager, n° 2470 OF Thursday 04/10/2007, p. 3.
[58] *Ibid.*

Many Cameroonians are therefore convinced that politicians, magistrates, journalists, teachers and religious can do much to reduce the level of corruption in the country. What can politicians do? For a politician to be useful in the fight against corruption, he must have been democratically elected by the people. It is necessary that he should really be chosen by his people whom he should respect and serve and who can control him.

Do our politicians - the Head of State, Parliamentarians and Mayors and their municipal counselors - have the necessary legitimacy to represent their people? I am not sure that all of them legitimately represent their people :" in the absence of an independent electoral commission, and in a situation where the electoral process has been vitiated at the base by an electoral code that allows the rulling party to be re-elected indefinitely, where persons who have been corrupted by the authorities in power do their best to make sure that the regime remains in power and where the helm of the state and the politicians all owe gratitude to the district and divisional officers, magistrates, civil servants, and other officials of public and private services who 'validate', approve and support the various fraud schemes in the electoral process"[59].

If we have the ambition to organize one day democratic and transparent elections, we must begin by revising our electoral code. The Bishops of Cameroon already proposed an electoral code which

[59] Pierre Titi Nwel, *Op. cit*, p. 78.

was considered inacceptable by the Minister of Territorial Administration and Decentralization. It is important for true democracy "that all political parties be convinced that power comes from God through the people"[60].

It is important for the politicians in Cameroon to know that "political power is not taken by force and is not maintained through cheating or violence." It is not conserved by physical, psychological or moral torture. A politician should also know that the political power he has is given to him for a while and will be controlled by God who gave it to him. One can say that our democratic process is seriously sick because its fundamental principles for political actions have been for long wanting, and sadly enough have continued to be so because the party in power has been there for years.

In all honesty, it can be said that "these political preconditions will have to be followed by a complete reform of the legal texts, which would give magistrates the power to apply the law freely and impartially. In this way the action of the media on public opinion will now be able to ask politicians to render account of their work"[61]. The religious also has a contribution to make for victory over this evil which threatens the very existence of Cameroon as a modern nation worthy of international respect. The religious should not wait "for these socio-political reforms to take place before they act"[62]. However their

---

[60] Ibid, p . 79.
[61] Ibid, p . 79.
[62] Ibid.

action has to be concrete and incisive, targeting not corruption in the abtract, which in fact is an idea against which it is very difficult or even impossible to fight, but specific acts of corruption carried out by well identified socio-professional groups"[63].

The model of the religious in her action is Christ who does not only denounce evil, but also stigmatizes the bad acts of those who could be classified among the socio- professional categories of the time: the scribes, the Pharisees, and the tax collectors. John the Baptist spoke directly to the tax collectors: " Don't make people pay more than they owe". " And to the soldiers he said, don't force people to pay money to make you leave them alone. Be satisfied with your pay"[64]. Also, " preachers should actively condemn the bad practices of those social actors whom the public considers as more easily prone to corruption: law enforcement officers, magistrates, teachers, health personnel, custom officers, vote holders as well as citizens who have reconciled themselves to it"[65].

He who makes known to men what the Creator who was, who is and who shall be wants to be done is like Ezekiel the prophet sent by the Almighty to warn evil doers and call them to conversion.

" If I tell the wicked man that he shall surely die, and you do not speak out to dissuade the wicked man from his ways, he (the wicked man) shall die for his guilt, but I will hold you responsible for his death.

---

[63] *Ibid*.
[64] Luke 3 : 13 - 14.
[65] Pierre Titi Nwel, *Op. cit*, p. 79.

But if you warn the wicked man trying to turn him from his way, and he refuses to turn from his way, he shall die for his guilt but you shall save yourself"[66].

Religious ministers in our context, that is to say the Imams, the Pastors, the Priests, have a grave religious obligation to warn he who corrupts or he who allows himself to be corrupted, of the gravity of his guilt. The salvation of the religious depends on this. The religious has the duty to make it   known to the one who corrupts and the corrupted, the moral gravity of their fault. In talking to them, he should call a spade a spade, and things by their names. The majority of those in our country who corrupt and who are corrupted are believers, they are men and women who go quite regularly to our churches and temples on Sundays, and to our mosques on Fridays. These men and women who believe in one God who will judge every one of us when we die, in relation to the good we did or the evil we committed. It is left to us preachers in our places of worship, to draw the attention of our faithful to the evil they do and what they should do to eradicate the evil of corruption which is destroying our country.

This evil makes our country a society: "of men who are like vipers to other men, of employees who not being contented with their wages shamelessly exact dues from the public, of heads of public and private institutions who, without any consideration for others take for themselves what belongs to all, or power hungry politicians who use government money to buy the consciences of the hungry"[67].

---

[66] Ezekiel 33 : 7 - 9.
[67] Pierre Titi Nwel, *Op. cit*, p. 79.

The religious man or woman should do every thing possible to bring about a radical change of the situation. We believe with Gerddes-Cameroon that: "accepted religions that are being practiced contribute in the forging of a social morality that can be taught. In this regard it is a powerful weapon in the fight against corruption"[68].

The teaching of human morality or ethics in our schools is important to fight corruption. To fight a vice the opposite virtue to it should be practiced. Because the situation in the country is grave and disquieting, the Bishops seriously draw the attention of all to it: let us have the courage, the determination, the will power to fight against corruption. The external signs and traces of corruption are perceptible. The material prosperity of certain individuals does not seem to be proportionate to their official revenue.

I know the case of a priest who refused to bless a house belonging to a young man that he knew. He suspected the origin of the money used to build the house. Was it stolen? I will like to say it again and again that Cameroon should use all political and judicial mechanisms that she has to destroy the structures of corruption in the country, the objective being to eradicate this evil which is a serious obstacle to our development. It is therefore important: " that all means of communication, public and private should, undertake and animate a permanent campaign against corruption"[69].

The Radio and the Television should regularly and rationally organize conferences and debates

[68] Ibid.
[69] Ibid.

interviews, documentaries on corruption etc. "Christians committed in the church and society - the laity, priests, religious men and women - should be the first to ask themselves questions about their relationship to money and to be involved in the pastoral ministry which fights against corruption"[70].

Also: "in our parishes, colleges, universities and schools the same method should be used to fight against corruption. Let all apostolic workers proclaim with courage the social doctrine of the church (...) and in particular the teachings of the church on the use of money and wealth. Let artists who are talented in the cinema, in theatre in dancing, in ballet, in singing and story telling, in poetry, in music, in carving and in painting, use their gifts in serving such a cause vital for Cameroon"[71].

The Bishops ask parents, who are the first to teach and to instill in their children essential Christian and human values of life, to incisively condemn before their children laziness, lies and hypocrisy; they should severely condemn fraud , deceit and stealing; "they should seriously correct their children if they commit such acts"[72]. The Bishops ask educators and teachers insistently, university lecturers, and those in charge of institutions of all levels, to do all that is possible to abolish corruption in schools and in universities, for the honour and the future of our country; let teachers incite in children love for"[73] work well done, the need for effort, respect for others their convictions and what belongs to them, the sense of the common good, generosity, and the spirit of service[74]. The good administration of certain Non

---

[70] *Ibid.*
[71] Pastoral letter of the Bishops of Cameroon on Corruption, n° 39.
[72] *Ibid.*
[73] *Ibid.*
[74] *Ibid*, n°42.

Governmental Organizations (N G Os) is an example for our administration and ought to stimulate our government in its fight against corruption.

May these organizations help us "to know for what they are the national and international institutions, the groups and persons guilty of corruption, and to denounce the fraudulent activities which compromise justice and peace in our country"[75].

The Bishops insistently demand "that the authors of corruption and those who embezzele government funds be brought to trial and judged according to the law, in order that our country might live in peace and security"[76]. They also say : "that the fight against corruption will not be achieved in a state where the legislative, the judiciary and executive powers are concentrated in the same person"[77].

They are also convinced that "a just revision of salaries and an effective control of prices, can effectively contribute to an efficacious fight against corruption"[78]. They also invite the state to apply article 66 of the constitution of Cameroon of 18 January 1996 on the declaration of property: "such a measure {...} would contribute to the ethics of good government and to transparency and would thus be an efficacious remedy against corruption"[79]. Furthermore, they make their opinion clear: "one of the effective remedies against corruption would be to create all over the country conditions that favour transparent elections"[80]. They are also "convinced that

[75] Ibid., n°43.
[76] Ibid., n°43.
[77] Ibid.
[78] Ibid., n°45.
[79] Ibid., n°47.
[80] Ibid., n°49.

the people should have the effective liberty to choose their representatives and to reject eventually those who did not govern well or embezzled state funds"[81]. In deed the Bishops are aware "that quite a number of citizens do the best they can at the price of many sacrifices to resist corruption. We thank God for what they are doing, and believe firmly that their example will influence others"[82], for the good of the whole nation.

We may summarize remedies against corruption as follows: " the elaboration of an adequate legislation and its effective application, taking dissuasive and punitive measures against those who go against the legislation, the real involvement of senior civil servants or those in power in the fight against corruption.(example comes from above) {...} Improving the level of workers and their conditions of work, simplifying procedures at the customs, education of citizens on their rights and duties, {...} the democratization of political structures of the country"[83].

---

[81] *Ibid.*
[82] *Ibid.*, n°51.
[83] Pierre Titi Nwel, *Op. cit.*, n°91.

5

The place of God in the building of a nation

The world belongs to God because he created it. He is a living God because he created living things, "but since the philosophy of illuminism, a part of the sciences wants to explain a world where God will be superfluous {...} and useless to our lives, but each time they seem to succeed things fall apart."[1] Indeed: " unless the lord builds the house the builder labours in vain who builds it. Unless the lord guards the city, in vain does the guard keep watch."[2] No people can be sure of its" future by undertaking the construction of huge buildings, by a sophisticated system of defense and by a well organized economy, without reference to God's"[3]; without reference to the supreme being who is simple, infinite, unique, immense and eternal. Nothing can be done without God.

Who is God ? It is not possible to define God. Every definition encloses what is defined within boundaries: now God has no limits, he cannot therefore be enclosed within boundaries. He is not finite. He is immensity itself. He cannot be measured. It is true that we cannot say who God is. But we can

[1] Benedict XVI, in Rome on 12/09/2006 during a political messager in the Company of numerous Cardinals, bishops, 600 priests, and 15,000 youths serving at the alter. More than 300,000 persons took part in the Islingenfeld square in Ratisborre.
[2] Psalms 127 or 126 : 1, in the Bible explained and commented : World Bible Alliance.
[3] Psalms 127 : 1.

prove that he is, that he really exist, that is to say that he exists objectively. Man cannot say who God is. But he knows that God is. St Thomas Aquinas proposes five proofs of the existence of God.

1- **The five proofs of the existence of God given by St Thomas Aquinas.**

The first proof concerns the movement of things.

Movement here does not only mean local movement that is to say movement from one place to the other, but in general, every passage from potency to act, that is to say every passage from a way of being to another way of being is movement. For example the transformation of a piece of wood into ashes is movement. In this proof of the existence of God from movement, St Thomas Aquinas is applying a principle according to which what is moved is moved by another. That is to say "nothing passes from potency to act without the influence of a cause already in act ; this means that nothing can be its own cause"[4].

In the light of this principle, St Thomas Aquinas shows that every movement has a first mover . It is evident he says, that certain "beings in the world are in motion. Now, every being that is in motion is moved by another. And it is not possible that a being should be at the same time what moves and what is moved, that is to say that it moves itself and passes from what it can be to what it is: (from potency to act). Therefore, if a being is in motion, it must be

---

[4] Regis Jolivet, Manuel of Philosophy, Lyon, Paris, Edition Emmanuel Vitt, 4è édition., n°1348 p. 293.

concluded that it is moved by another. That if, the being which moves is moved at the same time, it would be necessary that it be moved by another, and this another moved by another. Now this can not go on endlessly for then there would be no first mover, and it would follow that there would be no other mover either, because the intermediary movers move only if they are moved by the first mover , just as the walking stick is moved by the hand. Therefore the existence of the first mover who is not moved by another is necessary. This first mover who is never moved is God"[5].

From this proof of the existence of an immobile first mover, the following corollaries can be deduced :

1- "The first immobile mover is infinitely perfect. Every thing that changes is not perfect, since to change is to acquire a new way of being, if therefore the first mover is absolutely immutable, that would mean that it lacks no perfection, it is the plenitude of being. In other words the first mover is pure act"[6]. Thus, "the first immobile being is spiritual because what has matter is corruptible and is essentially imperfect. The first mover being spiritual is therefore intelligent and free, because intelligence and liberty are essential properties of every spiritual being"[7].

[5] Regis Jolivet, *Op. cit*, p. 293.
[6] *Ibid*, p. 294.
[7] *Ibid*, p. 295.

2- "The first immobile mover is eternal because he is absolutely immutable"[8].

3- "The first immobile mover is present every where because being the principle of the universal movement he is present by his power in every thing that moves, that is to say in the entire universe"[9].

The second proof: Causality.

In this second proof of the existence of God St Thomas Aquinas uses the proof which establishes the relationship between a cause and its effect. In the proof based on the movement of beings St Thomas Aquinas looks at the movement of being from the point of view of phenomenal becoming. In the second proof he looks at things from the point of view of causality: "what ever is produced is produced by another (other wise what is produced would be the cause of itself that is to say anterior to itself, and that would be absurd). From that we conclude by exclusion of endless regression, that there is a first cause which is the source of every causality"[10]. This first cause transcends and dominates absolutely all the causal service. The first cause can not be a cause like all the others in a series of causes: "in fact if the first cause were only a first element in a series of causes, it would be necessary to explain how this first element started to be a cause, that is to say that, by virtue of the principle that nothing can produce itself, it would be necessary to look for a cause anterior to the cause that is being considered to be the first and that is contradictory"[11].

---

[8] *Ibid.*
[9] *Ibid.*
[10] Regis Jolivet, *Op. cit,* p. 296.
[11] *Ibid.*

In the third proof... St Thomas Aquinas wants to prove that God really exists from the fact "that the physical world is made of contingent beings ; that is to say beings that are capable of not being. Now beings that are but are capable of not being, can not themselves explain their existence. In fact a being which is capable of explaining its own existence, that is to say whose nature is such that it can explain its own existence would exist necessarily, and always, it would have neither beginning nor end. This is not the case with contingent beings. The origin of the existence of contingent beings can therefore be only explained by the existence of another being, if this other being is also contingent it would need another being to explain the origin of its own existence. But this cannot continue infinitely: we are therefore obliged to draw the conclusion that there must be a being whose nature is such that it does not need another being to explain its own existence. This being is a necessary being. It exists by itself. It cannot not exist. It is that which explains the origin of every contingent being. This necessary being which exists per se, (by itself) and cannot not exist, is God"[12].

The fourth proof: here. St Thomas Aquinas uses the degrees of perfection to be found in beings."Various aspects of beauty are found in beings: if beauty is found in beings in different degrees, it must be produced in them by the same cause. It is impossible that this quality present in so many beings and in different degrees should belong to the nature of this

---

[12] *Ibid.*

being, other wise one would not understand why beauty would be found in them... The fact that there are different degrees of beauty, implies that the different beings in which these degrees are found share in a beauty which is outside and above this hierarchy of beauties and this beauty must be absolute and infinite"[13]. And this absolute and infinite beauty is God.

Proof number five: Proof of the existence of God from order in the universe. St. Thomas Aquinas says that : "the world is seen as some thing well organized where beings, as different as they may be in their natures, have a common purpose, which is the good of the universe. Now, that order is intelligible only if an intelligent principle exists, which organizes all things in view of their ends. {...}. It is therefore to be concluded that there is a cause outside the universe which organizes order in the world"[14]. This cause is God.

Any of these five proofs suffices to prove the existence of God. It is not therefore necessary to use the five proofs at the same time to prove that God exist. "Each of the proofs alone leads us to God and implies the other proofs. Thus to talk about the first immobile mover, is to talk about absolute perfection, a being that is not created and is eternal, is to talk about a universal cause"[15].

But there is some difference between the five proofs: each one stresses an aspect of the divine

---

[13] Regis Jolivet, *Op. cit*, p. 296.
[14] *Ibid*, p. 298.
[15] *Ibid*, p. 305..

causality and shows that, what ever may be the point of view that may be adopted, the existence of the world can not be explained without God, so much so that choice can only be made between the two following conclusions: either God or total absurdity.

St. Clement of Rome says this so well when he writes "the heavens, as they revolve beneath his government, do so in quiet submission to him. The day and the night run the course he has laid down for them, and neither of them interfers with the other. Sun, moon and the starry choir roll on in harmony at his command, none swerving from its appointed orbit. Season by season the teaming earth, obedient to his will, causes a wealth of nourishment to spring forth for man and beast and every living thing upon its surface, making no demur and no attempt to alter even the least of his degrees. The same laws sustain the deeps of the abyss and the untold regions of the under world. Nor does the illimitable basin of the sea, gathered by the operations of his hand into its various different centers, over flow at any time the barriers encircling it, but does as he has willed it - for his word was, ' Thus so far shall you come; at this point shall your waves be broken within you.' The impassible ocean and all the worlds that lie beyond it are themselves ruled by the like ordinances of the law. Spring, summer, autumn and winter succeed one another peaceably; the winds fulfill their punctual duties, each from its own quarter, and give no offence; the ever flowing streams, created for our well being and enjoyment, offer their breasts unfailingly for the life of man; and even the minutest of living creatures mingle together in peaceful accord"[16].

---

[16] Saint Clement of Rome, office de lectures, in Lithurgie de heures, TIV, p.214.

2- The nature of God

It would seem that the five proofs of the existence of God "helps us to know in some way, not only the existence of God but also his nature"[17].

We may ask ourselves what is the nature of a thing or of a being. It is "all the characters taken together to situate a thing or a being in a species or in a determined category"[18]. The chemist for example would ask himself what is the nature of the poison that caused the death"[19].

We could ask ourselves : Is it possible for us to know the nature of God ? The answer is affirmative. Just as we can know a cause from its effect we can also know God from his effects. " An effect always resembles its cause that is why our knowledge of the nature of God is possible and real. From our knowledge of what God has created, we can know the nature of God. But this knowledge of the nature of God is not perfect because to know a thing perfectly is to know the thing as it is in itself"[20].

We can therefore affirm categorically that man is able to know God. Because the imperfect knowledge that we have of God is all the same true. Scientific knowledge of the world is imperfect and inadequate; all the same it helps us to have some true knowledge of the world and its laws. In the same way if we can not embrace the Cameroon mountain we can all the same have some knowledge of it by looking at it.

---

[17] *Ibid*, p. 301.
[18] Paul Foulquie, Dictionary of Philosophical language, Paris, PUF, 1969, p.468.
[19] *Ibid*.
[20] Regis Jolivet *Op. cit*. p. 309.

God can be known. The book of wisdom says "all men were by nature foolish who were in ignorance of God, and who from the good things seen did not succeed in knowing him who is, and from studying the words did not discern the artisan; but either fire, or wind, or the swift air, or the circus of the stars or the mighty water, or the luminaries of heaven, the governments of the world they consider God. Now if out of joy in their beauty they thought them gods, let them know how far more excellent is the Lord than these; for the original source of beauty fashioned them. Or if they were stroke by their might and energy, let them from these things realize how much more powerful is he who made them. For from the greatness and the beauty of created things the original author by analogy is seen. But yet for these the blame is less; for they indeed have gone astray perhaps, though they seek God and wish to find him. For they search busily among his words but are distracted by what they see, because the things seen are fair. But again, not even these are pardonable. For if they so far succeeded in knowledge that they could speculate about the world, how did they not more quickly find its lord"[21].

But man knows that his knowledge of God is not perfect and this helps him to avoid errors: he should not think that the nature of God could be compared to his own. According to Regis JOLIVET : "we do not make God to our likeness". God has all perfections that are found in the things he has created, because the perfection that an effect has cannot be less in its

[21] Sg 13 : 1 - 9.

cause (that is to say an effect can not be more perfect than its cause) but the perfections in the effects are relative because they are mixed within perfection (effects are relatively perfect) when we attribute to God perfections found in things he has created we have to deny from those things what limits them and raise of them as infinite"[22].

This means that we attribute analogically to God the perfections that are found in creatures, for example intelligence, liberty and goodness are not only found in a superior degree in God than they are in man, but their presence in God is of another order"[23].

3- The attributes of God

The attributes of God are the perfections of God "that can be known by human reason"[24].

They are "the different aspects of the perfectly simple essence of God. There is no difference between them: they are divided into attributes that concern the nature of God and attributes that concern the activity of God[25]. Attributes that concern the nature of God:

a-The simplicity of God:

God is a simple being that is to say, he is not made up of parts. He is not composed. If he were composed, he would not be perfect because what is composed "depends necessarily{…}on the parts that composed

---

[22] Regis Jolivet *Op. cit.* p. 309.
[23] *Ibid.*
[24] *Ibid.*
[25] Regis Jolivet op. cit. p. 311.

it. If God were composed, he would be, in relation to the parts which composed him, a second being, a derived being . Now God is a being that is absolutely first. Therefore he can not be a composed being. He is therefore perfectly simple"[26].

b- The infinity of God:

God is infinite, he has no limit. " His nature is to be"[27]. It is difficult to see from where what limits him could come, "since there is nothing above him which depends on nothing and every thing that is, depends on him. The limitation of God could not come from himself, from his own will, because God did not make himself. Finally the limitation of God can not come from his essence or from his own nature, because his essence or his nature has all perfections and excludes all imperfections and limitations"[28].

c-The uniqueness of God:

This means that there is only one God and "this results from the fact that the idea of two beings infinitely perfect is contradictory. {…} If there were many gods, they would necessarily be different one from the other. Now this difference between them would imply that what one of them has the other does not have. None of them would therefore be absolutely perfect. And in that case none of them would be infinitely perfect that is to say none of them would be God"[29].

---

[26] *Ibid.*
[27] *Ibid.*
[28] *Ibid*, p. 312.
[29] Regis Jolivet *Op. cit.* p. 312.

d- The eternity of God:

God possesses totally and perfectly life that has no end. There is therefore in God neither the past nor the future; God is perpetually present. If God had a beginning, he would not be perfect. Now a beginning can not be attributed to a being that is infinitely perfect without being absurd"[30]. The attributes that concern the activity of God, are those "of spiritual beings that is to say: the operations of the intellect and of the will"[31].

In what concerns the intelligence of God, Paul Foulquie has this to say: "in God every thing is absolutely perfect. In God every thing is absolutely infinite. It follows logically that God is an infinite intelligence; that he possesses infinite knowledge, that he knows not only what was, what is. or what shall be, but all that is possible"[32]. The author underlines that: "God knows in his essence the infinite number of beings that he could create, that would share in his essence"[33].

We could now ask ourselves what could be the object of God's knowledge: the first object of God's knowledge is his essence which is always present in the divine thought with which God identifies himself. The second object of God's knowledge is all beings which are and which could be. "He knows them as more or less images of himself"[34]. How does God

---

[30] *Ibid.*
[31] *Ibid*, p. 313.
[32] *Ibid.*
[33] *Ibid.*
[34] *Ibid.*

know these things. To know a thing God does not need to reason like a human being. " Reasoning is an imperfection, it helps us to know a thing step by step and supposes ignorance. With a glance God sees every thing intuitively and his thought penetrates the inmost part of every being"[35].

4 - The activity of the divine will.

Let us now look at the activity of the will of God which is one of the two activities of a purely spiritual being, a being which has no body. It is important for us to underline here that the will " is an inclination towards a good that had been apprehended by the intellect"[36].

This inclination exists in God and makes God to love the good he knows. We may now ask ourselves: what is the object of the divine love? The answer to the question seems evident : the object of God's love is first and foremost God himself.

Indeed: "God loves himself as he knows himself. He knows himself to be infinite. He is absolutely the perfect good, which cannot not love and in the knowledge of which he finds his infinite happiness"[37].

The second object of God's love is all beings created in his image and likeness. In fact as far as our reflection on the will of God is concerned, we should know that God can do what he wants. His will has no limit.

---

[35] Paul Foulquié, *Ibid*, p. 313.
[36] *Ibid*.
[37] *Ibid*.

The study of the attributes of God "shows how limited we are and how incapable we are to know God as he is {...} And there is the highest point in our efforts to know God since by that we recognize the infinite transcendence of the being that has nothing in common with the other beings of creation"[38].

5 - God and the world

The world is all that is created by God, God is clearly different from the world, but he is "present in every being"[39]. That is to say, what ever exists, exist because of the continuous influence of God on it. This divine person in every thing that is, is spiritual. He is not bodily. The presence of God in every being should not make us to forget "the absolute independence of God in relation to the world and his authority on the entire universe"[40].

If God were not present in beings created by him, he would be a stranger to the world. Consequently, he would neither be infinite nor perfect ; and if God were not the sovereign lord of the world and absolutely independent in relation to the world, he would be identical to the world, and he would appear to be imperfect, potential and in becoming.

6- God is a personal being endowed with the faculties of intellect and will.

All that we have said obliges us to draw the conclusion that if God is, and he is, he must be a Being who has no limit, is infinite, "radically distinct from

---

[38] *Ibid.*
[39] *Ibid*, p.319.
[40] *Ibid.*

the universe which he has created and which he conserves by an act of free will"[41]. He must be a personal being, a being endowed with reason, conscious of himself and master of his acts. God must be a person, if he is the cause of beings endowed with intelligence and liberty; the creator of a being that is a person must himself be a person.

Who is God?

Judging from what precedes one should not be ashamed to ask the question. It is normal because one should always try to understand.

De Broglie, one of the greatest contemporary theoreticians of the problems of light has written: " what knowledge should we have, if we knew what a ray of light is " and a great Biologist, Jacob of Uexkull underlines : " every one of us knows what life is"[42].

Where is the difficulty of the reply ? When one asks: "what is light or what is life ? Or again: who is God?" The difficulty is not in the words *that, life , light or God.* However, we know what these words mean. But what makes the intelligibility of the interrogative proposition difficult is the word "is". What does the word "is" mean? If you do not understand the significance of the word every thing else remains enigmatic or mysterious and difficult to understand.

There is in Christianity a big division concerning the word "is". In the new testament written in Greek, during the last super with his apostles before his passion, Jesus gave them bread saying : "take and eat

[41] *Ibid*, p. 320.
[42] http :/haution. philosophie.pagesperso - orange.fr/Textes/Vie.htm.

this is my body." Taking the chalice filled with wine he said : "take and drink this is my blood". Catholics and orthodox Christians believe that the verb "is" in this context, can only mean that Christians eat and drink at holy communion the body and the blood of Christ. When the priest repeats the words of Christ during mass there is a substantial change of the bread and wine. Visibly they look like bread and wine but their substances have been transformed and become the body and blood of Christ.

The Protestants have another interpretation of the verb "is": the verb signifies for them that bread at communion symbolizes the body of Christ and that, while remaining only ordinary bread it has another importance, just as a ring increases in value for the one who receives from the hands of a beloved one.

The fact that thousands of books have been written on this subject shows that the word "is" is not as simple as one would think. Christianity has not been negative in relation to cultures before it. As we know, Christianity has incorporated in her way of thinking Greek philosophy, especially the philosophy of Aristotle.

Christianity has taken the concept of a God, who, himself unchanging, is the cause of all the changes in the world as St. Thomas Aquinas has shown us. It would seem that Aristotle has said that God is in the strict sense of the word. Humanly speaking it is difficult to think of a being that moves others but does not move. What is static can not be active. The motor of a machine has its own movements. To a motor is applied another notion : a motor is, but it also moves.

In his *critique of knowledge*, Kant writes: "the verb to be is not a real predicate {...} In logic it is only a copula or a link in a judgment. To say that God is good or just presents a sense. To say that God or another being is, is to remain in the domain of futility"[43].

When we ask ourselves what the verb to be means, the answer is that a being exists only as some thing that is becoming or evolving, or changing gradually over a long period of time. Eraclitus has said that every thing is flowing {panta rheil}. Paraphrasing what Eraclitus said one would say that one can not bath one's self twice in the same running stream. One cannot even bath in the same stream once, because in that once, while one is bathing the body and the stream change. Every thing, especially living beings change continually and make themselves new again.

How can the cause of the movement of every thing that moves not be able to move? If the images of God could give us an idea of the reality, the most faithful image of the father would be that painted by Michael Angelo on the ceiling of the sixtine chapel in Rome, which shows God flying in the storm. Also in this sense the book of Ruth shows clearly the wings of God .Those who say that God is not do not know that well known Christian Theologians long ago have said the same thing but gave it its true explanation. John Scott in fact writes : "literally God is not because he transcends beings. "And St Thomas says: "Divine

---

[43] Emmanuel Kant, Critique de la Raison pure, Paris, Puf.

being, which is the substance of God is not the common being. It is being different from any other being. The divine esse {Latin: to be} is not the common esse"[44].

Also, the word "to be" is not only a substantive or noun but is also a verb. No created being can only be expressed by a substantive, because it evolves, it is moved, and has a history. We can not apply the category "is" in a limited sense of having a fix state, to creation and much less to God the creator. When we say that God "is" we have said already too much about him.

The name of God in Hebrew is El, which expresses a relation. El signifies towards, the movement of the Alpha towards the Omega. The right translation of the name of God which he revealed to Moses Ehjeh, Asher EHJEH is *I will be what I will* be. King David the psalmist asked himself who God is and he replied ; "on a cherubin he flew, he flew on the wings of the wind"[45]. The Bible tells us that God flies but angels do not fly but come". In another psalm it is said : "he made his chariots from the clouds. He walks on the wings of the wind"[46]. From there comes the difficulty of answering the question "who is God"?

[44] Thierry Dominique Humbrecht, Theologie negative et nous divins chez Saint Thomas D'Aquin, Paris, J.Vrin , 2005, p.542, et suivant.
[45] Ps 18 : 10.
[46] Psalms 104 : 103.

6

The creation of the world

1- What does it mean to create?

To create means to make some thing out of nothing. Only God can make something out of nothing, "because to create something out of nothing requires power that is infinite"[1]. There are two possibilities that concern the origin of the world: "either God created the world absolutely from nothing or he made it from a part of his own substance"[2].

The world could not have been made from a part of the substance of God. That would be absurd and contrary to reason. "God is a spiritual being and therefore perfectly indivisible." A spiritual being is not made up of parts. It is simple. It cannot therefore be divided. God is a simple being. "He could not therefore create from his substance a material world composed and perishable"[3].

We are therefore obliged to conclude that God made the world absolutely from nothing. He could not have created the world from a substance that existed before the world. From where could have come such a substance? Either God created the world absolutely from nothing or from his own substance.

---

[1] Jolivet Régis, *Manuel de philosophie*, Lyon-Paris, Edition Emmanuel Vitte, 4è éd., n° 1398, p. 293.
[2] Paul Foulquié, *Op. cit.*, p.322.
[3] *Ibid.*

The opinion that he created the world from his own substance being absurd we conclude that God created the world ex nihilo, that is to say from nothing. We now know for certain that God exists and that the world is because God is. If the world exists it is because God wanted it to be, it is because he wanted to create it. He did not create the world because he needed it. God does not need the world to exists. Every thing in the world belongs to God and depends on him. He directs the world and knows what he is doing. And he alone has autonomous existence[4].

Man may reject God or may believe that God does not exist but that is a destructive serious mistake on his part. Whoever does not want to be under the authority of God calls upon himself evil, chaos, destruction and unhappiness as proclaims a hymn of the divine office: "all beings those that speak and those that do not speak proclaim God. All beings those that reason and those that do not reason pay him homage. Every thing continues to be by his power. The movement of the universe subsists by his power. He is the end of all beings. He is in all beings without totally identifying himself with any of them. He is not one of them, and he is not all of them put together. He has all names but how will I call him, he alone cannot be named? He is beyond all things"[5].

It is God who increases what we are and what we have. It is he who directs the life of man with wisdom and justice. He is the God of truth and fidelity to his word, "he is the rock, his work is perfect, for all his

---

[4] Walter Elwell, *Le Petit Guide de la Bible*, Forel, Maire-la-Vallée, 1984, p.144.
[5] Hymne de la Liturgie des Heures, vol III, p.554.

ways are equitable a trustworthy God does no wrong, he is the honest, the upright one"[6]! He has made man little less than a god, he has crowned him with glory and beauty, made him lord of the works of his hands, put all things under his feet , sheep and cattle , all of them, and even the wild beast, birds in the sky, fish in the sea, when he makes his way across the ocean"[7].

The psalmist says: "May Yaweh be a stronghold for the oppressed, a stronghold in times of trouble! Those who revere your name can rely on you, you never desert those who seek you, Yaweh"[8].

God does not like evil, he detests all evil doers and exterminates liars and hates the man who tells lies and sheds blood, protects those who love him, blesses the man who avoids evil and does what is good.

God is the inconceivable, the incomprehensible and the invisible. But all the same one can say that God can be perceived, understood and seen ; to see what he has created is to see him who is in action in every being ; it is to see he who is difficult to describe and who gives immortality to man who is mortal and "sustains the universe in being"[9]

God is faithful to the faithful, he does not blame the man who is without blame: He is loyal to he who is loyal. He gives us strength for all wars, makes our enemies surrender and gets us out of all quarrels.

God is the final end of human history, the point

---

[6] Deut 32, 4, in *Bilble de Jérusalem*, Cerf, Verbum Bible, 1995.
[7] Ps 8, 6-9.
[8] Ps 9, 10 - 13.
[9] Saint Irenée de Lyon, *Office des Lectures* du 28 juin, in *Lithurgie des Heures*.

towards which converges the aspirations of man, of history, and of civilization, the center of the human race, the joy of all hearts and the total fulfillment of their desires[10].

Every thing belongs to God: "all forest creatures are mine, the animals on the mountains in their thousands I know every bird in the air, what ever moves in the fields is mine. If I am hungry I shall not tell you since the world and all it holds is mine"[11].
It is he who has made man in his image ; it is he who has made darkness light. To him all is day. It is he who gets out of death new life. It is this God the creator of all that was, is and shall be who from on high and from far away follows our acts and hears our thoughts.

This God who is infinite is master of the law that gives joy to the heart, and life to all. By his power the simple become wise, his laws are just and his commandment is clear or transparent. His "decisions are just and truly equitable and more desirable than gold"[12].

His wisdom made all that we see: " the immensity of the sea and its many animals big and small that can not be counted, all types of birds, the earth and the mountains , the beast of the forest, man for whom all we see is made: from earth he gets his bread and wine that makes him happy, oil that smoothens his face and bread that strengthens his body "[13].

---

[10] *L'Eglise dans le monde de ce temps*, Paris, Centurion, 1967, 1012p.
[11] Ps 49, 10 - 12.
[12] Ps 18.
[13] Ps 24.

It is the wisdom of God that made all these things: the earth filled with all that is good. Every being depends on him. Every being is because he is. If he is not all that we see is not: "plants, animals and man receive their food from God at the right time." All life comes from God who is the light, that is to say: who is the end of every being. God who is simple, a being that is absolutely first, makes mockery of a wicked man, cares for the good man, "knows the days of a man of integrity who will receive an imperishable heritage"[14]. When God who is absolutely perfect guides our steps himself, they are firm and pleasing. Thus if the just staggers and falls, "he does not remain on the ground for Yaweh holds his hands"[15].

"From one man, this being without limit made all peoples so that they might inhabit the surface of the universe. He made them so that they might look for him and try to enter in contact with him and find him, he who is not far away from each one of us. Indeed it is in him that we live, move and are. We are of his race and he has fixed the day when he will judge the universe with justice"[16].

This God is the father of orphans and the defender of widows[17]. Despised, he despises no one. Scorned, he honors. He directs with wisdom and justice the life of men[18]. He "has deposed the mighty from their thrones and raises the lowly to high places. The hungry he has given every good thing while the rich he has sent empty away"[19].

[14] Ps 36,18.
[15] Ps 36, 23-24.
[16] Acte des Apôtres 17, 15. 22-18,1.
[17] Ps 67, 6.
[18] Ps 91,7 - 8.
[19] Lc 1, 51- 53.

We should know that this unique God "made us and we belong to him, we his people the sheep of his flock". He "is above all gods". "In his hands He holds the depths of the earth and the summit of mountains belongs to him; to him belongs the sea, it is he who made it and the earth. And that is why all his works bless him.

His angels bless him ; the heavens,
The cloud of the sky,
And all his armies bless him.
The sun and the moon
The stars of the heavens,
The showers and rain bless him.
Breezes and winds fire and heat,
Cold and heat bless him.
Showers and dew, frost and cold bless him.
Frost and snow night - time and day, darkness and light bless him.
Lightening and cloud and the earth bless him.
Mountains and hills, all plants of the earth,
Fountains and springs,
Rivers and seas, creatures of the sea bless him.
Every bird in the sky, wild and tamed bless him.
Children of men, priests of the lord, servants of the lord bless him.
Spirits and souls of the just, the holy and humble of heart bless him.
May he be blessed, the lord in the heavens, to him the highest glory and honor for ever[21].

This God the creator of every being is clothed and dressed with magnificence "
Is clothed in majesty and splendor,

[21]Cantique des trois enfants, Dn 3.

Wearing the light as robe!
He makes the cloud his chariot,
Slinging on the wings of the wind,
He makes the winds his messengers,
And flaming fires his ministers.
He fits the earth upon his foundation,
With the ocean as with his garment he covered it; above the mountains the water stood,
At his rebuke they fleet at the sound of thunder, they took to flight; as the mountain rolls they went down the valleys to the place you have fixed for them.
He did not set a limit they may not pass, nor shall they cover the earth again.
He sends forth springs into the watercourses that wind among the mountains, and gives drink to every beast of the field, till the wild asses quench their thirst.
Besides them the birds of heaven dwell; from among the branches they send forth their song.
He waters the mountains from his palace; the earth is replete with the fruit of his works.
He raises grass for the cattle, and vegetation for men's use, producing bread from the earth, and wine to gladden men's hearts, so that their faces gleam with oil, and bread fortifies the hearts of men.
He made the moon to mark the seasons ; the sun knows the hour of its setting.
He brings darkness, and it is night; then all the beasts of the forest roam about; young lions roar for their prey and seek their food from God.
When the sun rises, they withdraw and couch in their dens.

Man goes forth to his work and to his tillage till the evening[22].

All this happens according to the will of the creator.
Without this God, the creator of all that is , without this God simple, infinite, unique , present in every being which he preserves by the continual action of his power, without this God who is eternal because he exist necessarily , man can absolutely do nothing.

Without God we can do absolutely nothing good for our country? We are in dire need of God to govern his people and to develop this part of the world he has created and given to us.

---

[22] Ps. 103, 1-23.

7

The place of man in creation.

Of all the beings that God has created, only man is created in the image of God. Man therefore occupies a unique place in creation: "he is in the image of God; in his own nature he unites the spiritual and the material world"[1], the visible and the invisible world. In the visible world only man can know and love his creator. "He is the only creature on earth that God has willed for his own sake, and he alone is called to share by knowledge and love, in God's own life. It was for this aim that he was created, and this is the fundamental reason for his dignity"[2].

"Being in the image of God the human individual possesses the dignity of a person who is not just something but some one. He is capable of self knowledge, of self possession and of freely giving himself and entering into communion with other persons"[3].

All that is visible on earth is created by God for man. "But man in turn was created to serve and to love God and to offer all creation back to God: what is it that is created, that enjoys such honor? It is man - that great and wonderful living creature more precious in the eyes of God than all other creatures!

[1] CEC, *Op. cit.*, n° 355.
[2] CEC, *Op. cit.*, n° 356.
[3] CEC, *Op. cit.*, n° 357.

For him the heavens and the earth, the sea and all the rest of creation exists"[4].

Man created in the image of God is both a bodily and a spiritual being. He is spiritual because he has a soul.

The soul refers to the inner most aspect of man, that which is the greatest value in him, that by which he is most especially in God `s image"[5]. The body of man is human precisely because it is animated by a spiritual soul {...}, through his very bodily conditions he sums up in himself the element of the material world , elements which through him are brought to their highest perfection and can raise their voice in praise freely given to the creator. For this reason man may not despise his bodily life. Rather he is obliged to regard his body as good and to hold it in honor since God has created it and will raise it up on the last day.[6]

The body and the soul are so intimately united "that one has to consider the soul as the " form" of the body : that is to say, it is because of its spiritual soul that the body made of matter becomes a living human body; spirit and matter in man, are not two natures united but rather their union forms a single nature"[7].

The catholic church teaches that the human soul is created immediately by God and not produced by the parents ; " the church also teaches that the human soul cannot die : it does not perish when it separates from the body at death and it will be reunited with the body at the end of time"[8].

[4] Ibid.
[5] CEC, *Op. cit.*, n° 363.
[6] *Ibid.*, n° 364.
[7] *Ibid.*, n° 365.
[8] *Ibid.*, n° 366.

God created man and woman: "he created them in perfect equality as human persons; and in their respective beings as man and woman. " Being man" or "being woman" is a reality which is good and willed by God: man and woman possess an inalienable dignity which comes to them immediately from God their creator. Man and woman are both with one and the same dignity, "in the image of God." In their "being -man" and "being- woman" they reflect the creator `s wisdom and goodness"⁹.

This God is neither man nor woman, he is pure spirit in which there is no place for the difference between the sexes: the respective perfections of man and woman reflect something of the finite perfection of God: those of the mother and those of the father and husband.

"Man and woman were made for each other - not that God left them half - made and incomplete - he created them to be a communion of persons, in which each can be help-mate to the other, for they are equal as persons and complementary as masculine and feminine. In marriage God unites them in such a way that they can transmit human life : by transmitting human lives to their descendants man and woman as spouses and parents cooperate in a unique way in the creator's work" ¹⁰.

1-   Why did God create the world?

God did not create the world to increase his happiness. He did not create the world to make himself perfect.

⁹*Ibid.*, n° 369.
¹⁰CEC, *Op. cit.*, n° 372.

He did not create the world to increase his glory. On the contrary "creatures came into existence when his key of love opened his hand"[11].

In his goodness God created the world to show his perfection. He created the world to show and to share his beauty with every being that is why everything that is, is beautiful. Thus: "the glory of God consists in the realization of this manifestation and communication of his goodness for which the world was created"[12].

God made himself known by creation to give life to all beings that live on earth: "the ultimate purpose of creation is, that God who is the creator of all things may at last become "all in all" , thus simultaneously assuring his own glory and our beatitude"[13].

God did not only create the world, he maintains it. He "does not abandon his creatures to themselves. He does not only gives them being and existence, but also, at every moment, upholds and sustains them in being, enables them to act and brings them to their final ends"[14].

Yes, God loves all that is. Nothing that he has created is disgusting to him. For, if he did not love a being he would not have created it. "How would any thing have endured if he had not willed it? Or how would any thing not called forth by you would have been preserved"[15]?

---

[11] *Ibid.*, n° 293.
[12] *Ibid.*, n° 294.
[13] *Ibid.*
[14] CEC, *Op. cit.*, n° 301.
[15] *Ibid.*

We are already dealing here with divine providence which means, "the disposition by which God guides his creation towards its perfection : By his providence God protects and governs all things which he has made, reaching mightily from one end of the earth to the world and ordering all things well. For all are open and lie bare to his eyes, even those things which are yet to come into existence through the free action of creatures"[16].

God is perfectly wise. This demands of him vigilance "over the world he has created, in order to realize the purpose for which he created it." [17]

God is infinitely good and his goodness demands that he protects the beings he created and which he loves. They are the fruits of his love. God is infinitely powerful and his power demands that he governs with sovereignty the works of his hands.

Providence is not a capricious and arbitrary action or an action taken without reflection. It is the action of a sovereign and infinitely wise will; it conforms with the nature of every creature : the action of which it is essential to orient the course of things for the good of all, such as giving every being its place and defining clearly its function in the universe.

The action of providence, except in the case of miracles, is based on the activity of creatures. Providence is every where. It is in all we see. It is in our lives and in the movement of our hearts. It is in the aspiration of our souls, it is in the desires for good. And we cannot talk of providence without a word on miracles.

---

[16] Régis Jolivet, Cours de philosophie, op. cit., n°231
[17] Ibid.

2- What are miracles?

A miracle is a marvelous event which provokes astonishment and admiration[18].

In general the cause of a miracle is not known. When it is said that an event is miraculous that means that what has happened can not be explained by an ordinary cause. In the strict sense of the word, a miracle is a fact sensible and extraordinary, produced by God outside the ordinary cause of events, or an extraordinary event attributed to divine intervention[19].

A miracle excludes all natural explanation. Miracles are possible. A miracle is the suspension of a natural law. God who is the author of nature is capable of suspending what he created from nothing. This contradicts neither his wisdom nor the fact that God does not change, since a miracle, even if it does not observe the law of sensible nature, enters in the total order, which is spiritual, and was forseen by God as an element of that order[20].

3- Evil

It must be admitted that the presence of evil in a world created by a God who is infinitely good poses a problem to man. There are those who believe that the existence of evil in the world shows that God and the reality of divine providence do not exist. What then should be said about the existence of God and

---

[18] Régis Jolivet, Cours de philosophie, Op. cit., n°232.
[19] N. Lemaître, M.-T. Quinson, V; Sot, Dictionnaire culturel du christianisme, Paris, Nathan, 1994, p. 195.
[20] Ibid.

the reality of evil in the world? To deny the existence of God and of divine providence surely does not solve the problem. On the contrary the denial of the existence of God, far from solving the problem of evil would only make it insoluble. In fact if the evils which make us suffer had no solution or compensation, the world would be certainly absurd, deprived of sense and radically evil.

If that were so it would be difficult to understand the physical order in the world[21]. There, where the physical order is found, is also found the moral order.

Evil must be meaningful and explicable. To solve the problem of evil it is necessary to make a distinction between physical and moral evil[22].

Physical evil belongs to the corporal order and is manifested by suffering. Moral evil is essentially the voluntary violation of the order willed by God. It is also called fault or sin. Physical and moral evils are not simply the absence of a good superior to nature but the privation of a good convenient to nature[23]. From the distinction between the two evils we draw the following observations:
¹none of these evils is natural. That is to say none of them can be put in the definition of nature.

God, the author of every creature desires only the good of what he has created. No nature as such includes moral or physical evil understood as the privation of moral or physical good proper to its nature[24].

[21] N. Lemaître, M.-T. Quinson, V; Sot, Ibid. p.195.
[22] Régis Jolivet, Cours de philosophie, Op. cit., n°234.
[23] Ibid.
[24] Ibid.

{2} A rational creature because of its being finite can sin , "and for that reason it can introduce in the world evil that comes from sin. But that capacity is not a necessity"[25].

Man is a free being and God who created him respects and guarantees his liberty. Man who commits a moral evil does that freely. He sins because he knows that what he is doing is sinful but he still does it[26].

{3} It is good to be free to do that which one's will presents to him as good. It is good to be in conformity with the divine order by acts that come from a free will, and thus to collaborate in some way in the creative action of God. It must be underlined here that man is not absolutely free since he can make a mistake in what he decides freely to do. But justice demands that he be the master of his act and of his choice, in such a way that in sinning he alone is responsible for the evil he has done and its consequences[27].

{4} God cannot be the cause of evil. Evil in the present world comes from the moral disorder to be found in man, and moral evil is the cause of physical evil. As St. Augustine says: evil is either sin or the consequence of sin.

{5} God can make what is evil to serve a good purpose: only that suffering would be absurd and absolute evil that serves no good purpose, which would be neither the expiation of a fault nor the

[25] Ibid.
[26] Ibid.
[27] Régis Jolivet, Ibid.,p.234.

condition of a good thing to be done . Thus physical evil or suffering can be a means of reparation and a source of merit. In sin God includes for the sinner a possibility to do what is good: The sin of man can help him to know his misery, to humiliate himself before God and to ask for his forgiveness[28].

[28] *Ibid.*

8

My social credo.

I believe that the good of every Cameroonian is necessarily connected with the common good of all which is "the sum total of social conditions which allows people, either as groups or as individuals, to reach their fulfillment more fully and more easily"[1].

I believe that in the name of the common good those who govern this country are bound to respect the rights of every citizen, are bound to allow him to realize his vocation and to exercise the liberties which are indispensable for the entire development of every human being[2].

I believe that the common good should be oriented towards the spiritual and material progress of every citizen.

I believe that the political authority which does not look for the common good of those it governs loses the legitimate reasons for its existence and should be democratically put aside.

I believe with the church that authority tends to go beyond its competence. Political authority often abuses its power over the population that cannot defend itself. If political authority becomes oppressive, should the population take up arms

[1] CEC, *Op. cit*. 1906.
[2] *Ibid*.

against it? We hope that such a situation will never arise in our country but if it did arise the catechism of the catholic church teaches that, if the people have to take up arms against a dictator, five conditions must be fulfilled simultaneously[3]:

1. There must be certainly, grave and prolonged violation of fundamental rights
2. All other means of redress have been exhausted :
3.Such resistance would not provoke worst disorders:
4. There must be founded hope of success;
5. It is impossible reasonably to forsee any better solution.

I believe that the common good consists of three essential elements which are : "respect for and promotion of the fundamental rights of the human person, prosperity, or the development of the spiritual and temporal good of the society; the peace and security of the group and its members"[4].

I believe that the dignity of the human person requires the search for the common good. That is why each and every Cameroonian must work hard so that the material and the spiritual life of every citizen becomes better.

1- The civil authority.

I believe that the civil authority of this country must make sure that those it governs, have the minimum necessary for them to live a life truly worthy of a being made in the image of its creator. To lead a truly human life man needs food, clothing,

[3] *Ibid.*, n°2243.
[4]CEC, *Op. cit.*, n°1925.

good health , work, an integral education which takes into consideration, not only his origin but also his final end and his right, to found a family[5].

I believe that when a political authority makes laws that are not just and that contradict the laws made by him who created all that is, or makes decisions that are against the moral order, in conscience the citizen is not bound to obey them. In such a case "authority breaks down completely and results in shameful abuse"[6].

I believe that Cameroon like every other society , would lack order if it had no men and women legitimately invested with authority and who would take care of our institutions and who would make sure that the common good were safe guarded. An authority which is not legitimately invested is in fact not a true political authority.

I believe that the origin of a legitimate authority is divine. Every authority comes therefore from him who is responsible for order in the world. That is why St. Paul tells us with certainty that "Every one is to obey the governing authorities because there is no authority except from God and so whatever authorities that exist have been appointed by God"[7].

I believe that if authority belongs to the order established by God, "the choice of the political regime and the appointments of rulers are left to the free decision of the citizens"[8].

---

[5] *Ibid.*, n°1908.
[6] *Ibid.*, n°1903.
[7] Rm 13, 1.
[8] CEC, *Op. cit.*, n°1901.

I believe that the rulers of the Cameroon of today and of tomorrow "should not be despotic but act for the common good of all Cameroonians"[9]. They should know "That authority is exercised legitimately if it is committed to the common good of society. To attain this it must employ morally acceptable means"[10].

I believe that successful political regimes in Cameroon must be chosen by the people. They must respect the principles of the state of law that is to say that state in which the law is sovereign and not the arbitrary will of those who govern the people. No body is bound to obey a law that is not just.

I believe that those who govern us should know that those they govern are beings endowed with the faculties of intellect and will and are therefore created in the image of God.

The dignity of man is such that it can never be alienated by any human authority. His creator has made him little less than the angels, "and crowns him with glory and honor. He has given him rule over the works of his hands putting all things under his feet: all sheep and oxen, and the beast of the field, the birds of the air, the fishes of the sea, and what ever swims the parts of the sea"[11].

I believe that those who govern and those that are governed are equals. In the building of the country those who govern can do nothing without those who are governed. Every one is important in the building of the country. Those who occupy important positions in the administration of the country need

[9] *Ibid.*, n°1902.
[10] *Ibid.*, n°1921.
[11] Ps 8, 6-9.

the services of the humblest servants in the same administration.

In deed they are obliged to work together to be more efficient[12]. They have to work together for the common good like parts of the same body: "the head is nothing without the feet nor are the feet any thing without the head. Even the smallest of our physical members is necessary and valuable to the whole body; yet all of them work together and observe a common subordination, so that the body itself is maintained intact"[13].

In a country like ours every body is important for the building of the nation. The rich is not more useful than the poor, both the rich and the poor are human persons, equally endowed with the faculties of intellect and will. The great and the small are both human beings. The differences between them are only ; an accident being what is added to the essence of a being and can be suppressed without changing the nature of the being.

The fact that all men have the same human nature is the philosophical bases for the mutual respect we ought to have for one another. Every human being is created for the good of all human beings and all human beings are for the good of every human being. That is why every citizen has to become a precious stone for the building of the nation. For this to be possible, the mind of every citizen " should be filled with every thing that is true, everything that is honorable, every thing that is upright and pure, every

---

[12]Saint Clément, in Liturgie des Heures, *Op. cit.*, Vol IV, p. 1150.
[13] *Ibid.*

thing that we love and admire - with whatever is good and praise worthy"[14].

We therefore propose to ourselves the practice of human virtues which are "the habitual and stable perfections of the intellect and will that govern our actions, order our passions and guide our conduct according to reason and faith"[15].

These stable perfections to do what is good and to avoid evil are: prudence, justice, fortitude and temperance. The human virtue of prudence "disposes our reason to discern in every circumstance what is truly good for us and to chose the right means of achieving it"[16]. The human virtue of justice "consists in the firm and constant will to give to others their dues"[17];

The human virtue of fortitude assures firmness in difficulties and constancy in the pursuit of what is good. It reaches even to the ability of possibly sacrificing one's life for a just cause"[18].

The human virtue of temperance, "moderates the attraction of pleasures, assures the mastering of the will over instinct and provides balance in the use of created beings"[19]. A temperate man directs his appetite towards what is good. He is discrete and does not leave himself to be controlled by the passions of his heart. We should not leave ourselves to be controlled by the immoderate desires of our

[14] Ph. 4, 8 - 9.
[15] CECA, *Op. cit.*, n° 378.
[16] *Ibid.*, n°380.
[17] *Ibid.*, n°381.
[18] *Ibid.*, n°382.
[19] *Ibid.*, n°383.

passions; we should master our appetite and be moderate. Every Cameroonian worthy to be honored should live according to these cardinal virtues, "under which all the other virtues are grouped and which are the hinges of a virtuous life".

A just and honest man, a man who loves the truth, the good and innocent man, is his own judge. He does not pretend to be virtuous. He pays more attention to his own moral evil than to the moral faults of others. A good man is not curious about the sins of others, he does not look for what is to be corrected in others but for what is to be corrected in him. He pardons others and condemns himself. He is rigorous with himself and understanding towards his neighbors. A good man does not look at the splinter in the eye of his brother but takes the log out of his own eye first.

We are not condemning here the correction of a brother, a correction which should be given with discretion and respect. A correction of a neighbor can be a delicate and fruitful expression of charity ; to correct is to love but to do so we should realize that we have our own weaknesses which could be more serious than those of our neighbors, correct them, before being concerned about those of our neighbor which could be less grievous[20]. The less we pay attention to our faults, the more we are curious about the faults of others. Thus we do not look for what should be corrected in our own behavior but for what should be criticized in our neighbor. Since we are not ready to ask for forgiveness for our sins, we are

---

[20] CECA, *Op. cit.*, n° 384.

always ready to accuse others. Each and every one of us has his or her faults[21].

Virtue which is the stable and firm disposition to do good and to avoid evil, permits us to give the best of ourselves to accomplish the good that we want to accomplish. The virtuous man tends toward what is good and avoids intensively what is evil. He looks for what is good and tries to put it into practice. He wants to be like God who wants that MAN, created in his image to be as perfect as himself and to leave on earth without committing the slightest evil.

Every virtuous man pays much attention to what ever he does. He fears evil and runs away from it. He recognizes the authority of God and this helps him to live in security. What he says gives knowledge. He thinks before saying a word and accepts criticisms. He knows that it is better to acquire wisdom than gold, intelligence than money, to leave modestly with the poor than to share great wealth with a proud man.

A good man avoids the company of the aggressive, does not change the place of the pillars put there by the political authorities to show the boundary of lands. He judges objectively, and replies frankly, and does not pay evil with evil, but the good for the evil done to him, does not accuse his neighbor without reason. He knows that it is better to be poor and to live a life of integrity than to be rich and dishonest.

---

[21] Saint Augustin, in *Lithurgie des Heures, Op. cit.*, Vol II, 14 semaine, p. 256.

He knows also that he will never succeed if he hides his faults; but he who denounces his faults is pardoned. He is confident even before death. He is generous because he knows that the man who is generous towards the poor will never lack anything. But the man who closes his eyes to the misery of the poor will be cursed by many[22].

2- In order to be good

What should we do to be virtuous? Man cannot be good without loving his creator, without being humble of heart, without hating hypocrisy. To be good is not to be arrogant, to be good is not to do what one does not like to be done to one's self.

If you avoid to commit abortion, you are good. If you do not abandon your authority over your child and that from his infancy you teach him the fear of the Lord you are a virtuous parent.

A virtuous man accepts all that happens to him as something good, as a gift from God, knowing well that nothing happens to us without God allowing it. Every good comes from God, and every evil, physical or moral is permitted by God. A good man is double dealing neither in thoughts nor in words. Duplicity in languages is a deathly trap.

A good man is ready to share with the poor even the little he has; he knows that what he has is for him and the poor. He is not talkative. Let us know that the tongue is a deathly trap. He who masters his tongue masters himself. A good man is chaste, he avoids

[22] Proverbe, 14, 26, 32; 15, 7. 28.31-32, 16, 19, 22, 25.28, 24, 24; 28, 6.13.27.

every moral evil against this virtue: "adultery, masturbation, fornication, pornography, prostitution, rape and homosexual acts"[23].

A good man does not forget the last judgment, the day when every man shall be judged according to his thoughts and his words and will be rewarded or condemned. Heaven and hell are not imaginary. They are realities that exist objectively.

A virtuous man is just and does not provoke division. He proclaims love where hatred reigns. He pardons easily. He promotes peace where disorder is to be found, he promotes the truth where error is to be found. He awakens faith where doubt arises. He gives hope where distress is to be found. He gives light where darkness is found. He produces joy, brings love and happiness where sadness reigns[24].

Such is the way to become the virtuous man that Cameroon needs to become a truly developed country.

[23]CECA, *Op. cit.*, n° 492.
[24] *Lithurgie des Heures, Op. cit.*, Vol. III, p. 748.

9

The root of every virtue is the love for our neighbor.

Love is the mother of all virtues. It is the soul of every virtue, and without love it is impossible to do what is good. In practice, love does not only forbid us to do to another person what we will not want others to do to us but demands that "you treat others as you will like them to treat you."[1]

Who is the other to be loved? The other can be someone who loves us or who does not love us. The other can be our friend or our enemy, to truly love is to love everybody, friend and enemy.

By a friend I mean someone I love and he loves me; a friend may be my brother or sister of the same parents. The friend of a young man could be a young woman with whom he has matrimonial intentions. There is also that love I will call patriotic, the love of a citizen for his country. It is that love which pushes citizens of a country to work hard, to sacrifice themselves for the good of their country.

True patriotic love can only be found in a country where the citizens, free and governed by equitable laws, are happy and united and do everything for the esteem of the affection for their fellow citizens.[2]

---

[1] Mt 7, 12.
[2] D'Hollach cité par Petit Robert 1, Paris, 1992, 1379.

For patriotic love to be possible it is necessary that the sovereignty of the country should belong to all the citizens and should be directly excised by the people. A democratic spirit and culture are necessary. It is necessary that those who exercise political authority be true nationalists who love to serve and not be served.

Love can be political, that is to say, that persons can love one another because they have the same political option, because they belong to the same political party. Love for the other person can be religious, that is to say, one can love somebody because they have the same faith in a power, in a superior principle in which their destiny depends and to which obedience and respect are due[3], the person is a Christian or a Muslim like me. Love for our neighbors could be tribal, regional or national. I love my neighbor because we are of the same tribe, of the same region or of the same nation.

All these reasons for loving our neighbors are good, where there is love God is there, but for a just man, it is necessary for him to love even the person who does not love him; it is necessary to love even the person who persecutes you and makes you to loose your employment. To love the person who hates you is surely a difficult thing to do but it is not impossible to do it. Love is the taproot of all virtues.

If each and every one of us loves his neighbor as he loves himself, what a beautiful country Cameroon would be? The Cameroon of our fathers will be a

---

[3] D'Hollach, *Op. cit.*

country where all of us will love to live. It would no longer be a country where the poor and the miserable are left to fend for themselves because every Cameroonian does not open his heart to the poor, to the sick, to those who have no shelter, to those who have nothing, to those who are thirsty, hungry. Every Cameroonian is my brother.

This country would be something else than what it is today if Cameroonians from north to south, from east to west, anglophones or francophones realized that we are brothers and sisters and capable of loving instead of hating, of unitirg instead of dividing, of practicing justice and peace instead of injustice and violence, of pardoning instead of naving the desire to revenge.

May it happen that everywhere in our national triangle, as journalist love to call our dear and beautiful country, be found security and peace; enemies reconciled, adversaries greeting one another, tribal groups and families accepting to walk together and love gaining victory over hatred[4].

National unity is to be found where there is brotherly love. In our relationship with our friends or enemies no bad word should come out of our mouth. If someone has something to say, it should be said in a constructive and acceptable way to those who are listening to us.

"Never let evil talk pass your lips; say only the good things men need to hear, things that will really help them. Do nothing to sadden the Holy Spirit

[4] Les Evêques du Togo, Prière pour la paix, que l'on fait à chaque messe. htt://ephata.actifforum.com/t2296-au-togo.

against the day of redemption. Get rid of all bitterness, all passion and anger, harsh words, slander, and malice of all kinds. In place of these, be kind to one another, be compassionate and mutually forgiving. Just say God has forgiven you in Christ"[5].

All Cameroonians are brothers; we shall cease to be brothers and sisters at the end of the world. When we shall cease to sing together our national anthem and have the same flag, we shall no longer be brothers and sisters. Despite our tribal and regional differences we are all brothers. None of us chose to be born in Cameroon; we did not choose to come together as a nation. We found ourselves together as a people with the same rights and duties.

A Cameroonian who does not accept another Cameroonian as his brother, as a gift of the creator to him, makes a big mistake. Let us together look for our common good. If every Cameroonian is concern only with what is good for him as an individual, our country will never become a developed country. One has the impression that we are a people where every one is concerned only with his own well being and does not look to the neighbor. Our national ambition -which should not be just a demagogical slogan - should be to look for the well being of every Cameroonian. If each and every one is happy all of us will be happy. If we aim at the good of every citizen, a prosperous future shall be assured for everyone of us in our country. A fight against every moral and physical evil in our society demands this new mentality, this conversion of the heart, this new way

---

[5] Eph: 4, 29-32.

of being Cameroonian. Everything is possible, the thief of yesterday could become a just man today. Every human being is capable of doing what is evil because of the fault of Adam and Eve. He is also capable of doing what is good because he is created in the image of his creator who is absolute goodness.

Let all we do be the expression of what is good: "whatever you do, work at it with your whole heart, do it for the lord rather than for men, since you know fully well you will receive an inheritance from him as your reward ; be slaves of Christ the lord. Whoever acts unjustly will be repaid for the wrong he has done. No favoritism will be shown"[6].

Let us not work to please man, this is difficult. It is easier to please God who forgives and forgets, than to please man who pardons but can never forget.

For the good of this country, each and every one of us needs a spiritual renewal, because what makes a man unjust comes from within him: "Wicked designs come from the deep recess of the heart, acts of fornication, murder, adulterous conduct, greed, maliciousness, deceased sensuality, envy, blasphehemy arrogance and obtrusive spirit".

"All these evils come from within and render a man impure"[7].

Nothing that comes from outside man makes him impure ; what renders us impure is the evil that is within us.

[6] Col 3, 23.
[7] Mc. 7, 20-23.

10

The place of God in our national life.

"Unless the lord builds the house he labours in vain who builds it. Unless the lord guards the city in vain does the guard keep vigil"[1].

We cannot do anything good for our country without its Creator. We should never forget God in all we do for the good of our country. Let us confide ourselves totally to God. Let us work hard in order to have enough food to eat or clothes to wear. But let us know that life is worth more than food and that the body is worth more than clothes[2].

Let us not look for what we are going to eat or for what we are going to drink, we should not be worried.

Indeed those who do not know God look for all these things unceasingly. God our creator knows well that we need all these things. Let us look first for the kingdom of God and he will give us all we need[3].

In what concerns the development of our country let us put all our confidence in God. Let there be no separation between the service of God and the search for what is necessary for our material well being. Let us work for the development of our country without

---

[1] Ps 127, 1.
[2] Mt 6, 25.
[3] Luc 12, 29-31.

forgetting that if God does not build our country with us we are working in vain to develop it. Let us confide ourselves to the lord and he will guide us.

Let us be of good behavior and confide ourselves to God. We should confide to him, our joys and sorrows. He will satisfy the desire of our hearts. Let us work towards him and he will act in our favor. Let us rest in him and count on him in every thing we undertake[4].

Without God, not only can man do nothing, but he ceases to be man. He is active because God is with him always. If God is not with us, we sink into oblivion or become nothing.

Our life is a sharing in the life of God; and to share in the life of God is to see him and enjoy his goodness; in seeing God we become immortal beings like him. It is God who gives being to every thing. It is God who maintains every thing in being, we leap because God leaps. Without God we can do nothing good for the building of our nation: "the life of man is the sight of God"[5].

Wisdom is of no use if God does not govern it, says the author of the imitation of Jesus Christ. God is the unique governor and the absolute authority of the world. That is why every human authority is only a sharing in the authority of God who alone is authority itself.

Every authority, even political authority, is of divine origin; that is why he who exercises human

---

[4] Ps 36.
[5] Sainte Irenée, in *Lithurgie des Heures*, Vol III, *Op. cit.*, p.1125.

authority should know that he is called to serve the people that God has confided to him. To govern a people is to serve the people. Every man who exercises authority over others should know that one day he will have to render account of how he governed them to him who is supreme authority. God is every thing to all. Without him, we can do nothing, without him we perish; without his support we have no strength to do any thing; his look suffices to give us courage and life. We shiver but he strengthens us; we are lookwarm, but God embraces us.[6]

God is the beginning of all that is. He is the end of everything. He makes sure that everything contributes to the good of those who love him. And if he is for us who can be against us[7]? Surely nobody. He is our light; of whom shall we be afraid?

If God is our strength before whom shall we tremble. If the wicked advance against us to destroy us, it is they our enemies that stumble and fall. "Though an army incamps against us, our heart will not fear, though war be waged upon us, even then we will trust him"[8], if he is with our nation and we with him. In all we do for the good of this country we should count on God. He is the king of nations.

---

[6] *Ibid.*
[7] Rm 8,31.
[8] Ps 26, 1-3.

11

A new Cameroonian.

A radically transformed Cameroon needs a new Cameroonian; a Cameroonian with the fear of God, a fear which is the beginning of wisdom, the source of life, the reward of humility and the fullness of wisdom[1].

This country needs political leaders that have the fear of God[2], and hearts that fear God[3]. A nation where those who govern and the governed do not know God and therefore have no fear of God is heading towards its political, economic, moral and spiritual auto destruction.

Our country would be good for all if every citizen leaves himself to be purified of all its moral weaknesses. That purification which is necessary for every citizen is not possible without the fear of God: a fear that is the expression of love and respect.

God alone is capable of giving to every Cameroonian a new heart and spirit. He alone can change our hearts of stone into hearts of flesh, hearts that love God and the neighbor[4]. God alone can give us those virtues which I call the virtues of a citizen: love for the country, love for work well done and

[1] Ps 110, 10, Pr. 14, 27, 22,4; Sir. 1,11-40.
[2] Ps 54, 20.
[3] Ps. 63, 17.
[4] Ez. 36, 25-27.

solidarity between citizens. Let those who govern us have favorable dispositions towards the poor, the rich and foreigners; let them be merciful towards those who are suffering because of violent and social injustice of every kind; let them be patient towards those who are strong or powerless and let them not condemn abusively any one.

All these virtues that we have just seen go to make up the crown of the Head of State ; without them authority on earth can not govern well[5].

1- The unity of all for the building of the country

I believe that for its development a people should be perfectly united, full of sympathy, brotherly love, tenderness, simplicity, should not render evil for evil nor insult for insult.

On the contrary let every citizen ask God to bless every other citizen. "How good is it, and how pleasant where brothers dwell at once"[6]; divided we fall, united we stand. Nothing is done by rivalry among those who are united; the one considers the other as superior to him, does every thing in humility in the spirit of communion, affection and compassion. The one sees himself as the mirror of the other, they serve one another; they have mutual respect for one another and do everything possible to avoid erroneous judgment[7].

There where unity is found is to be found also love for work well done; there where unity is found is to

---

[5] St Etienne de Hongrie, in *Lithurgie des Heures*, VIII, *Op. cit.*, p. 1246.
[6] Ps133, 1.
[7] *Cf.*, Ph 2, 1-5.

be found also perseverance in work well done; there where is to be found unity of heart and of the spirit, discipline, intellectual, humility, purity of heart and body are present. Everything is possible for a nation whose soul is unity. Without unity, as long as every Cameroonian does not feel at home every where in Cameroon, this country will never be a nation, but a conglomeration of tribes, not complete independence. Our state seems to approve and to encourage the present political situation.

2- What Cameroon for our children?

I believe that the Cameroon of our children should be a country where fundamental values of social justice are scrupulously respected. These values are truth, justice and liberty. Truth as a value of social life, of life in common amongst men, is the agreement between what one says and what one thinks. What one says is the verbal expression of one's thought. "Men and women have the specific duty to move always toward the truth, to respect it and bear witness to it"[8].

"Justice is a value that accompanies the exercise of the corresponding cardinal virtue"[9]. This social value is very important for our present society "where the individual value of the person, his dignity and his rights are seriously threatened by the wide spread tendency to make exclusive use of the criteria of utility and ownership"[10]. To promote justice is the obligation of all ; to listen to the cry of the poor, of the

---

[8] CDSE, *Op. cit.*, n°198.
[9] *Ibid.*, n°201.
[10] *Ibid.*, n°202.

minorities, of women not respected in their dignity, of the marginalized, of badly paid employees, of refugees, of immigrants and prisoners,[11] is our duty.

The third value of social life, liberty, "is the call, rooted in reason and will, to act or not to act, to do this or that, and so to perform deliberate irresponsibility"[12].

The more we do what is good, the more we become free. The ultimate good of liberty being God, "as long as freedom has not bound itself definitely to its ultimate good, there is the possibility of choosing between the good and evil."[13] But to choose to do evil is to abuse one's liberty.

A man who is free is responsible for his voluntary acts. Every man has therefore the natural right to be recognized as a free and responsible being. The right to exercise liberty cannot be separated from the dignity of the human person. This right has to be recognized and protected within the limits of the common good and public order. Since in the exercise of one's liberty the common good and public order must not be ignored, it can be said that man, in his relationship with other men is not absolutely free. His liberty is finite and fallible. Only God is absolutely, infinitely and infallibly free to do what he wants because his will is free from all limitations. God can do what he wants except what implies contradiction; what is contradictory being nothing and by not being able to limit in reality the all powerful divine might.

---

[11] *Instrumentum Laboris*, II Synode pour l'Afrique n°62, 2009.
[12] CDSE, *Op. cit.*, n°1731.
[13] *Ibid.*, n°1732.

The Cameroon of tomorrow will make sure that every citizen and his liberty are respected. That is why "neither his life nor the development of his life nor his goods, nor his personal and social activities can be subjected to unjust restriction in the exercise of his rights and freedom"[14]. Every authority in our country will have the duty to make sure that the liberty of every citizen is guaranteed. Is a woman free to eliminate her baby or to abort? Provoked abortion, the expulsion of a fetus or the interruption of conception before its term, is seriously elicit; it is murdering somebody, an act grievously against the moral law. You shall not kill.

Provoked abortion as an end or a means, is an abominable crime. God has confided to the woman, a noble ministry or the priestly ministry of life. She has to carry out this ministry with dignity. She should even be ready to make the supreme sacrifice of her life so that the child she has conceived lives. She has to choose in case of any complication at child birth the life of the child and to confide her own life to God who alone is the master of all lifes. Everything possible should be done to save the life of the mother and the child. And if in doing so it happens that one or both of them die, there is no crime there. The life of every Cameroonian like that of every human being should be respected and protected absolutely from conception to natural death.

Liberty is respected when every member of our society is allowed to realize his personal vocation, to look for the truth and to profess his religious, cultural

---

[14] CDSE, *Op. cit.*, n°133.

and political ideas, to express his option, to choose his state of life and as far as possible, to choose his profession, to take economic, social and political initiatives[15].

To practice these fundamental social values of truth, justice and liberty, "is the sure and necessary way of obtaining personal and a more human social existence. They constitute the indispensable point of reference for public authorities called to carr yout substantial reforms of political, cultural and technological structures and the necessary changes in institutions"[16].

We dream and we have the right to dream, for a developed Cameroon, where every citizen will have the minimum material goods necessary for him to live a life worthy of a human being.

We are dreaming of a Cameroon whose political leaders will be holy men and women. Yes! He who created us wants us to be holy men and women. A Head of State can become a holy man. A member of parliament can become a great saint. In October 2009 during the special synod of bishops for Africa, when it was announced that the procedure for the beautification of Julius Nyerere the former president of Tanzania had started, all the bishops present gave a standing ovation as if to say we were waiting for this.

There are examples to imitate in the political history of the world: Saint Venceslas King of Bohemia and Thomas More Chancellor of the king of England.

[15] *Ibid.*, n°200.
[16] *Ibid.*, n°197.

King Venceslas was a man of authority in a kingdom of immorality; he was very charitable towards the poor, he protected widows, he loved everybody, the rich and the poor, friends and enemies[17].

Saint Thomas More was a lay Christian father of a family and a great writer, Chancellor of King Henry VIII ; he was also a man of culture and led an ascetic moral life. He was condemned to death by Henry XIII for having refused to ratify his divorce and to recognize the king as head of the Church of England. These two personalities, King Venceslas and Thomas More truly served their countries. Thomas More said that he would prefer to abandon all his goods, his property and even his life "than to take an oath against his conscience"[18]

Our country can have politicians convinced that in every situation they can strictly apply the following ethical principles: to do what is good at all cost and to avoid evil whatever sacrifices may be demanded of them. The Head of State or a politician can become a saint. Dream of a developed Cameroon with me! No human being alone has all that is necessary for his material and spiritual development.

As far as the development of the individual and of the community is concerned every Cameroonian needs his brother or sister: The young need the old and the old need the young; the strong need the weak and the weak need the strong; the poor need the rich and the rich need the poor. Talents are never equally distributed. These diversities encourage us and oblige

---

[17] *Lithurgie des Heures*, Vol IV, *Op. cit.*, p. 1018.
[18] *Ibid.*, p. 1110.

us therefore to be generous: "they foster the mutual enrichment of cultures"[19]

In our country is to be found "grave inequalities. The economic inequalities amongst us are a scandal. And this scandal is always shocking every time we hear those who govern this country repeat the same promises to the people year in year out as if the person has a short memory! Amongst us Cameroonians there should be the practice of charity and solidarity. Our social and economic problems will be solved only with the application of solidarity in all its forms: "solidarity of the poor with the poor, solidarity of the rich amongst themselves, solidarity of the employer with the employee"[20], solidarity between tribes and solidarity between regions. Without this principle of social charity, a people can not consider itself a nation. That is why the insertion in our Constitution of the concept of indigenous and non-indigenous is a scandal. These are articles which should absolutely be abolished from our Constitution instead of trying to modify the Constitution to make some citizens stay eternally in power.

What ever may be the nature of the help that we receive from outside the country it will never be developed if its citizens have not cultivated the habit of hard work. The foundation of the family, the first human society is work. "It is work that assures the means of subsistence"[21] and guarantees the education of the child. Work in the farm in a country like our own merits particular attention; because of the

[19] CEC, *Op. cit.*, n°s1936-1937.
[20] *Ibid.*, n° 294.
[21] *Ibid.*, n° 299.

cultural, social and economic role it continues to play in the economic systems of many countries[22].

The work of man has two dimensions: objective and subjective dimensions. The objective dimension of work is "the sum of activities, resources, and technology used by men and women to produce things, to exercise dominion over the earth in the words of the Book of Genesis"[23]

The subjective dimension of work "is the activity of the human person as a dynamic being capable of performing a variety of activities that are part of the work process and correspond to his personal vocation. The subjective dimension of work is more important than the objective dimension, "for the subjective dimension of work is that of man himself who does the work while determining its quality and highest value"[24].

---

[22] CDSE, *Op. cit.*, n°270.
[23] *Ibid.*
[24] *Ibid.*

12

The Christian and the development of his country.

Whatever we do, we who are baptized, we should act like Christians. I believe that a Christian has a cardinal role to play in his country. He ought to be the light and the salt of his country. As light, he shows to all, by the good example of his life the way towards the good to be done for the building of his country. As salt of the land he helps his fellow citizens to avoid the evils which undermine the political and socio-economic life of his fatherland.

Our country will begin to develop, when we who believe in Jesus Christ without whom man cannot do anything good, realize that the solution to our problems is not only to be found in democratic elections well organized, but especially in putting into practice the word of God. The word of God tells us what we should do in all situations.

A Christian should know that his religion is the fundamental principle of life, the soul of the world, the principle of unity of all men. If in Cameroon we do everything possible to practice what the word of God tells us to do or avoid, corruption, bad administration of the common good and hatred will disappear. We will live as brothers and sisters. Our progress will be integral in all we undertake to do for the good of our country.

Where are they today, those countries that want to develop without God, what God has created and confided to them? If Europeans are today the scientific, technological and economic leaders of the world it is thanks to the Christian religion which they put into practice in a certain period of their history. Do you know that the United States of America was founded by Christians who came from England: the 'pilgrim fathers'? We know that all the universities of the 13 century, the Sorbonne in France, Oxford in England and Bologne in Italy were founded by the church? It is the church that preserved European culture from being destroyed by the barbarians who wanted to destroy that civilization which was very much linked to the Christian religion. Let us do the same thing in the development of our country. That is why it is strange that European political leaders refuse to make mention in the treaty of European Union of the Christian roots of their continent.

It is very necessary that Heads of States should know the central truth of the world: God alone governs the world. He is the soul of the world. Because God is the world is, and will continue to be.

It is impossible to govern Cameroon well without God. The word of God is the corner stone of liberty and makes of those who live it attentively, good citizens, good ministers, good fathers and mothers of families[1], and good agents of development.

There is no wall between God and the state. Those who govern us are children of God and servants of the people. One day they will have to render an

[1] Georges Grant, *The Changing of the Guard*, Broadman & Holman,Nashville (Tennessee), 1995, p.35.

account of their administration, not to those who elected them but to God himself. A Head of State, a Minister, a Governor, or a District Officer will render account of his work to God face to face.

Somebody can have a political vocation: it is God who called Gideon to the political ministry[2]; it is God who called Debora to the service of the city[3]; it is God himself who called Samuel to serve the people[4]; it is God who made David a famous king[5]; it is God who made Joshua a politician[6]; it is God who made Nehamiah[7] and Daniel politicians. All these heroes well understood that we can serve God by serving man in the political life and militate in the party of one's choice, on condition that all we do is done according to the will of God.

Nothing in itself is evil. It is man created free who can make bad use of his liberty. A Head of State can be a great servant of God and of the people he governs. If the God who created the universe is with him he will succeed as a political leader, his country will progress socially, economically and morally during his term of office. He will have the joy to see his people happy. But a bad Head of State who identifies himself with "visionaries and militants of erotic revolution(...), who have deformed the reality, nature, culture, tradition, authority, a state of law, the image of the father, morality, religion, truth, good and evil, reason, conscience, objective knowledge, individual personality, personal happiness, eternal

[2] Jg. 6, 11-14.
[3] Jg. 5,1-7.
[4] 1Sam. 3, 1-19.
[5] 1Sam 16, 1-13.
[6] 2Roi 22,1.
[7] Neh 1,1-11.

life, immortality, the love of neighbor, friendship, replaces (...) spiritual progress by regression, reason capable of discernment by negative reason (...) spiritual love by narcissistic love, moral conscience by lack of conscience, imagination and sensuality"[8].

A Christian politician should know that what he does could be an answer to the truth which saves, an answer to the truth that God alone rules the world he created. Political action for a Christian is not the forceful control of man. Man is an animal that reasons. In all we have to do with man we should reason and dialogue; force should never be used when we are dealing with a human being. Authority is natural and of divine origin. That is why the use of authority implies neither the use of force nor the use of constraint. On the contrary where force is used it can be truly said that authority has failed.[9]

Also authority does not need persuasion like arguments or debits to prove its existence. That is why Hannah Arendt has rightly said; the essential characteristics of authority "are that those from whom obedience is expected recognize it unconditionally; in this case it needs no constraints nor persuasions (...), authority is maintained only when the institution or the person exercising it is respected"[10].

We should underline here that a Christian politician in all he does as a politician should make

[8] Marguerite A. Peeters, La Mondialisation de la révolution de la culture occidentale. Concepts-clefs, Mécanisme opérationnels, Bruxelles, Institute for Intercultural Dialogue Dynamics, 2007.
[9] Hannah Arendt, La crise de la Culture, Paris, Gallimard, 1972, p.123.
[10] Hannah Arendt, Du mensonge à la violence, Paris, Calmann-Levy, 1989, pp.145.146.

known to the other person the goodness of God by usus pedagogus, usus motivatus, usus normativus[11].

The Christian believes that we need good law makers. He believes that we need good judges and good administrators in a country like our own. But this is not enough.

It is also necessary that those who govern us have faith in Jesus Christ, the Messiah and only mediator between God and man. Thus what the .Christian politician should do will be the recognition of and a submission to the will of God, the legislator par excellence. To act with God in politics is to give God what belongs to him; it is especially a manifestation of the grace of God in the life of a politician[12]. The christian, is the salt of the earth and the light of the world we repeat; "thus because of the commitment of the laity in political life the Christian whether he be teacher, businessman or civil servant, security agent or politician, should be a witness to the good, the true and the just and the love of God in his daily work or in what he does daily"[13].

The faithful of Christ, salt of Cameroon earth, should do everything possible to preserve our country and its inhabitants from the evils of hatred violence, injustice and tribalism. He should, as a Christian, purify and cure the spirit of all lives and of hearts, of all corruption and diabolical ways, in order to keep alive the country and its people, while preserving them in the road of rectitude and the social values of reconciliation, justice and peace.

---

[11] Georges Grant, *Op. cit.* p.35.
[12] *Ibid.*
[13] Jean Paul II, *Ecclesia in Africa*, n°86.

What is important is that the symbol of salt invites the lay faithful of Christ in Cameroon to leave himself to be consumed for the life of his people[14]. The Christian is also light wherever he lives and works. To be light where he lives is for him a call to be connected in the name of Christ, a call to be witness to the light of the knowledge of the gospel of Christ[15] lived, celebrated and prayed. The Christian is truly the salt and the light of where he lives and works, if he helps people to learn to live together, in their social inter communal life, how to dialogue together for peace there where families are divided, there where there is tribal misunderstanding[16].

The Christian is the salt and the light of his country if where there is violation of the rights and duties of man he supports by his words and by his commitment, the security and liberation of the victims[17], who works to make the society democratic and promote good administration of goods and persons, the culture of giving without expecting anything in return[18]. Where the state exploits the people, he is the salt and light of our national triangle and helps to build a better future for our children.

Let the Christian, disciple of Christ and therefore salt and light of our world, serve the just and ensure equal distribution of goods and equitable access to

---

[14] Synode des Evêques, II Assemblée spéciale pour l'Afrique, Relatio ante disceptationnemn, Cité du Vatican, 2009, p.14.
[15] Ibid., p.16.
[16] Jean Mbarga (Evêque du diocèse d'Ebilowa), Intervention au Synode spécial pour l'Afrique, octobre 2009, Cité du Vatican.
[17] Ibid.
[18] Ibid.

employment, where people are without work, without health facilities, without sources of revenue.[19]

The Christian should do everything possible to mobilise everybody for peace, for just and transparent elections, where there is war, rebellion often provoked to have access to authority or to remain in power at all cost[20].

A Cameroonian Christian as salt and light of his country would be the prophet, the advocate, the intercessor in favor of laws, social structures enlightened by a Christian humanism[21].

The Christian, salt of the earth and light of the world, should be a mediator who tries to reconcile antagonistic parties, does what he can to prevent conflicts and animate permanently social dialogue[22].

A Christian is a citizen of this country like any other Cameroonian. He has the same language and the same culture with those who belong to his tribe. He lives in the same village or town like other Cameroonians. He does not use any extraordinary dialect. His way of life is not particular. He is dressed like everybody else, does what is his duty as a citizen like every other Cameroonian, marries and bears children like any other Cameroonian family. But what is the difference between a Christian and someone who is not a Christian?

A Christian lives in the world but he should know that he is not of the world. The Christian lives on earth, he is a citizen of a country on earth, but he is

[19] Bishop Mbarga Jean, *Ibid.*
[20] *Ibid.*
[21] *Ibid.*
[22] *Ibid.*

especially a citizen of Heaven. A Christian should obey all laws of his country that are just?

The Christian should love everybody even if everybody does not love him, even if everybody persecutes him. People can say things evil about him but he forgives. He blesses those who insult him, he finds his glory when he is being despised; outraged, he honors. Such is the substance of letters to Doignete, the Christian in the world; he is not different from the other men. He lives in the same country, has the same language and customs like his fellow citizens. They do not have their own towns. Christians do not have an extraordinary dialect. Their style of live is the same with the others. Their doctrine is not the discovery of the imagination of the dream of a spirit that is worried; they do not pretend to be champions of a doctrine that is of human origin.

They live in great cities and in the cities of barbarians according to the destiny of each of them; their clothes are the same with those of others, their food and the rest of their existence, while at the same time they show the extraordinary and truly paradoxal laws of their way of living. Each and every one of them lives in their own fatherland as strangers.

They carryout their duties as every citizen and accept all difficulties like strangers. Every foreign land is their fatherland but they do not abandon their new born. They take place on the same common table but which is not an ordinary table. They are in the world but not of the world. Their life is spent on earth but they are citizens of Heaven. They obey human laws, but their way of life is more perfect than what the laws demand. They love everybody but everybody persecutes them. They are not known but they are condemned; they are killed and it is thus that they find life. They are poor but are rich. They lack everything but have everything in abundance. They are colonized but they find their justification. They are insulted but they are blessed. They are outraged but they honor.

When they do good they are punished as if they were evil doers. When they are blamed they are as happy as if they were born to life. Jews organize wars against them as if they were strangers, and the Greeks persecute them; those who detest them cannot say why they are hostile to them.

In other words, what the soul is to the body the Christians are to the world. The soul is to be found in every part of the body as Christians in the cities of the world. The soul lives in the body, and never the less it does not belong to the body, as Christians live in the world but do not belong to the world. The invisible soul is held prisoner in the visible body, thus the Christian; they are seen to live in the world but the worship they give to God is invisible. The body detests the soul and wages war against it, even though the soul has done nothing against it, but because the soul prevents the body to enjoy all pleasures; in the same way the world detests the Christian for no reason, but because the Christian opposes its pleasures.

The soul loves this body and its members that detest it as the Christian loves those who detest him. The soul is in the body and maintains the body; the christians lives in the world as if in a prison but it is he who maintains the world. The immortal soul camps in a mortal tent: thus the christian also camps in the corruptible world while waiting for the incorruptibility of Heaven. The soul becomes better by mortifying itself by hunger and the test; and the persecuted Christians multiply themselves day by day. The place that God has fixed for them is so beautiful that they are not allowed to desert it.

Our country urgently needs to renew itself, to transform itself radically. This supposes a new Cameroon, a Cameroon where God is at home in the hearts of those who govern, in the hearts of those who exercise even the least authority. We will never repeat enough the saying that all authority comes from God to serve man who has as his final objective, eternal life. If we do not build this country with God, we work in vain. Nothing good can be done without him to whom every man owes his life and all he has. Looking back retrospectively in the history of those countries which wanted to exclude God from their civilization, we see clearly that to want to build a country without God is to want to work in vain and that is something against nature or unworthy of man created in the image of the lord.

Let every Cameroonian who loves this country, ask the all powerful only one thing to give to every Cameroonian, a new heart ; thus shall we build a country where we shall live as brothers and sisters, to develop this small part of this world, while doing what is good and avoiding what is evil, even if we are the only ones to do it.

Conclusion

What should I say? Not much. My intention was to contribute to the emergence of a new Cameroon where Cameroonians radically transformed, having become very aware of the existence of God, live according to his principles.

God is able to give to every Cameroonian, especially to our political leaders or to those who aspire to become political leaders, the grace, the wisdom and all the virtues of a citizen which would allow all to live together. These virtues are the fear of the lord, the love of neighbor, the love of one's country, the love of work well done, the transparent administration of public affairs, the refusal to do what is evil in act and in thought, the building of peace. Let those who govern us listen to the cry of those who are suffering and try as much as possible to help them in their suffering. Let them no longer be indifferent to the cry of orphans, widows, street child, and of the anguished of those who do not know what tomorrow has for them. Let them be merciful to those who are suffering because of violent and social injustices, and let what they do conform to the prescriptions of God. Let them not forget in what they do daily this interpellation of God, "where is your brother Abel? What have you done? Listen! The blood of your brother cries towards me from the earth".[1]

---

[1] Genèse 4, 9-10

Let every Cameroonian young and old remember these words of Victor Hugo: "the future belongs more to the heart than to the spirit. To love, is the only thing, which occupies and fills eternity. To the infinite, man should be given what cannot be exhausted. Love shares in the nature of the soul. It is of the same nature with the soul, like the soul it is a divine spark. Like it, it is incorruptible, indivisible and imperishable. It is a point of fire which is immortal and infinite, that nothing can limit and that nothing can quench. Its burning is felt up to the marrow of the bones and its rays are seen to go up to the farthest point of the sky(…) ; what love begins can only be ended by God[2]. Many of my fellow compatriots will be surprised to see me write again another book. I'm convinced that the souls are not touched only by words. Those who do not have the occasion to see me every day also have the right to know what I think. It is also in thinking about the future generation that I always say that everyone knows that the spoken word flies but the written remains.

Secumo Hilary has said; every lasting change for the good of the majority of citizens of a society, has no means of avoiding the determining phase of the conscientisation of its beneficiary actors. That is why a man who is educated who does not think of writing, is like a piece of land that has received good grains but is deprived of a catalytic element to make the seeds to germinate. It practically limits its action, its influence on its immediate surrounding and on the length of its own biological existence.[3]

[2] Victor Hugo, *Les misérables* 1, Paris, Livre de poche, 1998, pp. 1062-1064
[3] Hilaire Sikounmo, *L'école du sous-développement. Gros plan sur l'enseignement secondaire en Afrique.*, Paris, L'Harmattan, 1992, p.34.

Annexes

1

In the name of all those struggling to survive

By Sebastien Mvogo

His Eminence, Monsignor Cardinal Tumi,
Father Bishop, peace and joy of Christ!

Chesterton once said, that what deserves to be done must be accomplished, even though only imperfectly. That is why I take upon myself the risk of sending you a long and unarranged letter, some paragraphs of witch might seem obscure to you.

Please, kindly sacrifice a moment, to read these pages and share the anguish I now feel over the fate that is mine and that of many downtrodden young Cameroonians, having no one to confide in.

This is a cry; it is mine, and likewise that of many young Cameroonians and Africans wondering what to do in order to survive. I would like to cry it out from all roofs, along all the roadsides, everywhere there are men and women of good will.

Say to all men of good will: "We are in a ghetto in our country",

I hurt, I cry out before you: Listen!

Listen to my feeble voice, so weak, yet sincere!

I cry out towards you: "Misery is killing us! Misery is killing me!

Can you hear my feeble voice, so weak, yet so sincere?

I cry out in the name of those hundreds of thousands of

young Cameroonians who must prostitute themselves to survive, and are already or will be victims of AIDS.

I cry out in the name of the great crowd of young Cameroonians enslaved and victims to misery, who work for a daily wage of 500 frs; the youth exploited by bosses more inhumane than some bosses of the last century; letting 16 years teenagers die in their fields.

I cry out in the name of all the young victims offered to the selfish pleasure of greediness.

I cry out in the name of all the young Cameroonians who suffer sickness, their handicap, loneliness and marginalization, all the youth unable to attend the Sunday assemblies because they are miserable, all the youth to whom no one dares to reach out in their misery.

Is it untrue that each person has the right to a place where he would feel at home, that he or she has also the right to a minimum of shared love?

Cameroon is under the dominion of the cult of money, sex and above all the exploitation of the weak.

Within our families, human life and the values of life are no more promoted: values of solidarity and sharing are replaced by individualism, pride and the exploitation of the weakest. Opinion leaders guide the masses toward divisions of all sorts, they even encourage and fuel the flames of hatred and unhealthy passions.

I cry out in the name of all the youth like myself, victims of violence, psychic harassments, all sorts of injustices, who live in great insecurity and who know not to whom we might turn for help, we who are submerged by loneliness, physical and moral. We the marginalized of a society sacrificed to the demons of money and sex.

Our country appears to be the only one in Central Africa that hasn't suffered the hammer of weapons, but peace is much more than the absence of war. Practical and philosophical materialism kills more than the bombardments of weapons. The exploitation of the weak is as cruel as a bomb blast.

Bossuet, a French writer and Prelate, explained it well: "Know that the oppression of the weak and innocent isn't the entire crime of cruelty: this crime has other aspects, because you haven't fed it, you have killed it; since you haven't clothed it, you have stripped it off. It is what makes us, sirs, murderers without shedding blood and thieves without stealing."

The Cameroonian government's institutionalized cruelty is very subtle, but also the most murderous and sadistic. We the majority of young Cameroonians have lost the taste of life, the courage to carry ourselves on, because we have become the dirt of the ruling system; a simple dirt. It would be better to live in a monarchy rather than African political systems. We are being killed slowly: it seems to me that it would be better to be killed once and for all rather than suffer the torture, both psychological and practical that we now go through in Cameroon.

Father Bishop, the Church must never remain silent, she must pass as retro, react, rather than be accused tomorrow of complicity with those who are guilty of the contemporaneous auto-genocide.

It seems to me that money lenders treat only with states. Meanwhile, states have but merely superficial understanding of the crucial problems of their people, or even seem to be intentionally unaware of them altogether.

When financing projects for example, no account is taken of those whom circumstances have favored less in the areas of education and wealth. The 30% personal contribution requirement is an effective obstacle among many others.

We wish to come out of the dumps, but for lack of means, we find ourselves in a dead end. If we are already unable to enjoy the luxury of feeding ourselves satisfactorily three to four days a week, I wonder how we might manage to save and capitalize 30% of personal contribution.

A question becomes imperious: we the disfavored in the areas of education and wealth, don't we have the equal right to improve our living conditions, to rise out of the mud in which we have been buried, to enjoy the solidarity of our leaders?

There are youth of humble backgrounds, shadows erring in this life, unable to build themselves up, disfavored by various painful circumstances; youth whose entire existence is filled with multiple financial obstacles. Don't they have the right to live?

Why not let the suffering I bear in my heart flow when even my very body testifies to my misery: 1m 72" on 48 kg? How can I ignore the enormous fear of tomorrow and beyond this fear the anguish that paralyzes me as my body itself testifies to my misery-induced pain?

We bear the mark of suffering on our face, we need help, but who can provide it for us? We doubtlessly may turn willingly to the local Christian community for help. Yet, on second thought, the truth is utterly otherwise: it is clashes among social classes, the crushing of the weakest, belittlement, spiritual pride. It is the faith of the little wealthy, it is the aggressive and inhumane answers that come as hammers out of mouths to further bury those hearts broken and traumatized by misery, in short, it is false charity: those whom the good Lord has spared from material poverty by keeping certain ills off their heads, take refuge in good inner dispositions toward others, as an excuse for their lack of practical charity, in actions. Each time a case of misery is presented within a community, rather than endeavoring to eradicate it, we hear words such as: you should pray! Not that prayer is secondary or less important, but it equally summons our human responsibility. Another commonplace expression is said with the same emptiness: "Each person carries his cross", forgetting Saint Paul's words: "Carry one another's burdens". Even though we may be unable to bear another's burden, we may help him to ease himself off, to ease himself off in us: it takes but only a minute to listen to him both kindly and attentively, in order that it might be in us even as it is in him. More often this listening of the heart is lacking in our local community leaders. Where then are love and charity? Saint James would say: "If a brother or sister has nothing to wear and no food for the day, and one of you says to them, "Go in peace, keep warm, an eat well," but you do not give them the necessities of the body, what good is it?" "My little children", adds Saint John "Let us love not in word or speech but in deed and truth." Authentic charity builds but on an authentic sentiment of love and kindness, and is realized by way of external acts of charity. Inner charity and practical charity are inseparable. Here at home, all is cast upon God and human responsibility toward the neighbor is ignored. Saint Thomas Aquinas has said: "A minimum of wellbeing is required to practice virtue". Those who offer us only prayer as an absolute recipe while withdrawing themselves from their responsibility to ease their neighbors' misery, do they even know that a weakened body cannot truly pray?

Of course, the paths of our earthly life are often filled with much difficulties, but too many extremely trying circumstances weaken the soul, and subject the spirit to rebellion against anything. And as for trying circumstances, there is too much in Cameroon. Cameroon is a radically miserable country, but this misery is not apparent: with about 10 million outcasts whose mute misery is in need of a fraternal help. A palpable example: during the June 2008 session, Cameroon had 37 thousand Baccalaureate holders. Out of the 37000, 10000 being unable to make it into advanced schools poured out into the streets. Out of the remaining 27,000, only 15% were able to move on securely with their studies, their future being secured since their birth (namely 4,050). The remaining 22,950 were abandoned to their own fate after two years at the University. Some are becoming alcoholic and drug addicts, others consumed with the fire of misery without anyone showing concern for their fate. Christians in my country have betrayed Christ, we have failed all along the line. How many youth do not join our Eucharistic assemblies because of their misery? They are suffocating not knowing who man is, what life is, their reason to live, and what to do with their life.

We are struggling to succeed, our efforts are unfortunately vain! The State is the facilitator no more, and we are even losing the vital speed. Men are born to be equal in rights, but we are never equal in rights: the community that welcomes us is itself already a community of inequalities.

The joblessness, the crushing weight of state structures, the financial instability, the affective emptiness, to which are joined all those who mock at us directly or behing our back, and you have Father Bishop the painting of a huge revolt, mine.

Animals, when they run out of provisions go out toward the areas where they might find what to survive by. If animals do as such, then what more of Man. When young Africans are criticized for leaving their country daring to challenge waters, are they not right in doing so? In fact, what has the State done for them?

Far from finding a way out, the fire that burns me from within becomes more ardent each day, I would be unable to hide the ever-renewed sufferings, the courage to struggle for life, and my patience fades out, while my desire to cope with the impasse grows.

To God alone I pour out my heart, of the misery that crushes me, since no one comes to my help. I turn over to you convinced of your commitment to stand for the sufferers in order that you may grant me your fatherly help, that I might regain my dignity that is threatened.

I would be grateful to you all my life for such a great act of charity; and that will enable me to testify, be sensitive to my pitiful condition, I would be grateful to you unto eternity.

The black man persecutes his brother, tortures and massacres him without sparing his children." This declaration by the reverend Jean Marc Ela can seem exaggerated.

My personal experience of suffering

When I remember all the difficulties I go through because of the wickedness of men and mostly those of my tribe, it is not exaggerated to say, the black man has but one goal: destroy his brother for his personal interests. To recount the whole terrible story of my life and origins calls for an unending essay, and I will return to it later on. For now, it is more convenient to focus on the subject matter of this letter.

To say the truth Father Bishop, the hope that is in me is but in scraps, I dare not say I am too tired to continue to live this way. I would hope that after reading this letter you help me find men of good will that will help me acquire three hectares of land around the vicinity of Yaounde. This piece of land will enable us, my co-sufferers and myself, to farm and improve our living conditions. In life there are two things that are immutable priorities: - To have a roof - Earn the daily bread. We can put on a single cloth all year round provided we make sure it is always clean. The needs in terms of clothing are not as urgent as being homeless or going without daily bread. The lack of food especially in the African continent where social welfare is absent, where States have nothing to do with the downtrodden is a scandalous matter: /man goes as far as even selling off his dignity in order of survival.

Who is writing to you?

I am a Cameroonian by citizenship. I was born on 06 December 1976, 103 kilometers away from Yaounde. I am from the Centre-South Province.

My father was a farmer, and my late mother also farmed. My father had but an only brother, this uncle was the elderst in a family of seven children delivered by my paternal grandmother.

My late uncle led an errant life: his occupation was carpentry. He died without being married. My father on the other hand, married my mother and had five children. Three died a few months after their birth. My younger sister and I haven't known a joyous childhood. My father would beat my mother up six days out of seven. This led to her early death. She died when I was eleven-year-old. But for the courage and goodwill of our grandmother, we would have died of hunger.

Like everyone, I too have sought happiness, I have sought a better life. As a teenager, when I entered secondary school in first year Accounting, I was sure to leave school benches as an expert accountant. I had the "traditional" schemes in my head. In fact, circumstances have proven that I was unable to achieve my dreams. My grandmother's death was disastrous, so much go that I was forced to quit the class of "premiere G2" during the school year without even the "probatoire".

I had nobody to motivate me. Had I any, in spite of all the pressures of the time, I would not have abandoned studies. In 1998 I abandoned studies, disgusted with everything and unable to pay even part of my school fees: school is not for the poor. I am sorry to say this but I have to say it: without money no one can study in the true sense of the term. Being unable to continue with studies I was

216

forced to get into active live. I succeeded in starting a poulting; with 100 chicks. When the business was to take off, we had the phenomenon of imported foren chicken cold chicken coming from Europe. This crippled all the small farmers and even some big farmers who then changed their economic activities. After this chicken rearing failure, I resolved while working on construction grounds on a salary of 1500 Fcfa a day to save 120000 Fcfa to buy a bail of used clothes : this business is a true lottery: it may happen that you fall on a good bail just like on a bad one. I had the misfortune as a beginner to fall on a bad quality bail. This failure was cruel and led me to many health issues: I was morally and physically broken. This led to violent headaches, stomach pains that I still have until now.

I abandoned trading and started seeking a job. God alone knows what looking for a job is in Cameroon, mostly for us who are without any expertise. From one misfortune to another, the last job dates back to May 07 at the "Assurama" insurance company which closed on June 07. With a 15000 francs salary a month and 10,000 francs transportation fee, a real exploitation of man by man: catechists' and irregular salaries; with all the responsabilities we are burdered with in life (rent, water, electricity, bread, health, etc.)

Listening to me, a question might cross the reader's mind: how can a farmer's son suffer this way? Why not go back to the village and cultivate the 40 hectares of land left by my late uncle and my late father?

One might even consider me a lazy person. Physical strength, I do not have as a robot, yet as a farmer's son and an authoritarian father would not be lazy. This being said, agriculture, I can do very well, it is an area where I excel. Only, I can't go back to the village because I have predators there: uncles from the extended family have one goal, to exterminate my father's family. In our culture, land ownership is more cultural than juridical, which explains how my father while dying left no land certificate and in order to make one now, a colossal investment is required; which I am unable to undertake now. At the time I speak to you, all that is left of the blood that gave me life, is my younger sister; two against a multitude! On three occasions I have been lynched to near death in my village ; the third time I collapsed. My persecutors thought I was dead ; were it not for a providential intervention, I would have died in the forest after two days without any strength to pick myself up.

Where does one lay his head in such circumstances? Death under bombings is less cruel than the way the system kills us in Cameroon: we are being killed slowly. One would like to see corpses laying by the roadsides to believe there is misery, but is not the gangrene in our society visible? How many do sell their very own bodies to have what to eat, how many trade their souls for the same end, how many buy the Advanced Teachers Training School certificate because they need to secure a stable job? There are many legion and that is the most atrocious of miseries: the moral misery, the misery of the conscience.

In the face of this anonymous cruelty we who have chosen Christ do not cease to wonder:

- How to be a witness to the gospel which is a message of freedom for the oppressed?

- How to assume ourselves?

Money and work are literally synonymous. For without work no money, so much so that, when you have no job you are considered by nobody, you loose your identity. When they ask: "Who is a so and so?" the answer is: "It is an executive, a trader, a teacher, and so on ; of course life does not come down to an occupation. One must confess nonetheless that the concept is indispensable for our psychic balance. Many questions arise:

- How to survive without falling into the temptation to compromise?

- How to help a young miserable like me stop thinking that his misery or his condition is a result of a fatality?

- How to continue believing that we are human beings with the right to live rather than a life of doom?

- How to establish the link between faith and the daily life problems of man?

- How to show this crowd of pessimistic miserable youths in the words of Monsignor Thomas Nkuissi that "Jesus Christ sets men free" when one himself is entrenched into serious survival difficulties? How may I even convince others that Christ is Savior, if not by serving them? How then put myself at their service if I am below the minimum?

- How to overcome without any resources the problems that society poses to the commitment of faith?

All these questions are to be answered by the young miserable Christian. All is vanity, but while we remain in our body, our nature is subjected to biological laws: eat, shelter, start a family...

The Christian should be poor and not miserable in the words of Baba Simon: "Misery is the enemy of God... to be poor, is rather fighting against misery, promote the culture of sharing... In short, we are crying for help, misery is killing us!"

We were telling you my story; I say we, for without the constant help of the Holy Spirit, I never could have written this letter to the end. For the time being the flame of hope that burnt in me is in scraps, shattering my life. In the world, other youths die everyday crushed at the very stage of their youth by a misery induced by the circumstances of life.

May the Lord grant to his Church of today evangelical communities who truly practice unity and sharing after the example of the first communities.

To people of goodwill, I plead for pity over my sad

condition, open your hearts and arms to me.

Father bishop, in a few pages this is my sorrowful story: deprived of the advantages of education and wealth, I have fought against misery and, until now, I have not been able to find my way to the sun. It is what leads me, Father bishop, to speak out to you asking the favor to be honored with your paternal assistance.

With an equal respect, father bishop, your very humble son.

The year two thousand and ten, the eleventh of the month of February, in the feast of Sainte Bernadette.

Universal Declaration
of Union Rights

Preamble

Whereas recognition of the inherent dignity and of the equal and inalienable rights of all members of the human family is the foundation of freedom, justice and peace in the world,

Whereas disregard and contempt for human rights have resulted in barbarous acts which have outraged the conscience of mankind, and the advent of a world in which human beings shall enjoy freedom of speech and belief and freedom from fear and want has been proclaimed as the highest aspiration of the common people,

Whereas it is essential, if man is not to be compelled to have recourse, as a last resort, to rebellion against tyranny and oppression, that human rights should be protected by the rule of law,

Whereas it is essential to promote the development of friendly relations between nations,

Whereas the peoples of the United Nations have in the Charter reaffirmed their faith in fundamental human rights, in the dignity and worth of the human person and in the equal rights of men and women and have determined to promote social progress and better standards of life in larger freedom,

Whereas Member States have pledged themselves to achieve, in co-operation with the United Nations, the promotion of universal respect for and observance of human rights and fundamental freedoms,

Whereas a common understanding of these rights and freedoms is of the greatest importance for the full realization of this pledge.

Now, Therefore THE GENERAL ASSEMBLY proclaims THIS UNIVERSAL DECLARATION OF HUMAN RIGHTS as a common standard of achievement for all peoples and all nations, to the end that every individual and every organ of society, keeping this Declaration constantly in mind, shall strive by teaching and education to promote respect for these rights and freedoms and by progressive measures, national and international, to secure their universal and effective recognition and observance, both among the peoples of Member States themselves and among the peoples of territories under their jurisdiction.

Article 1.

- All human beings are born free and equal in dignity and rights. They are endowed with reason and conscience and should act towards one another in a spirit of brotherhood.

Article 2.

- Everyone is entitled to all the rights and freedoms set forth in this Declaration, without distinction of any kind, such as race, color, sex, language, religion, political or other opinion, national or social origin, property, birth or other status. Furthermore, no distinction shall be made on the basis of the political, jurisdictional or international status of the country or territory to which a person belongs, whether it be independent, trust, non-self-governing or under any other limitation of sovereignty.

Article 3.

- Everyone has the right to life, liberty and security of person.

Article 4.

- No one shall be held in slavery or servitude; slavery and the slave trade shall be prohibited in all their forms.

Article 5.

- No one shall be subjected to torture or to cruel, inhuman or degrading treatment or punishment.

Article 6.

- Everyone has the right to recognition everywhere as a person before the law.

Article 7.

- All are equal before the law and are entitled without any discrimination to equal protection of the law. All are entitled to equal protection against any discrimination in violation of this Declaration and against any incitement to such discrimination.

Article 8.

- Everyone has the right to an effective remedy by the competent national tribunals for acts violating the fundamental rights granted him by the constitution or by law.

Article 9.

- No one shall be subjected to arbitrary arrest, detention or exile.

Article 10.

- Everyone is entitled in full equality to a fair and public hearing by an independent and impartial tribunal, in the determination of his rights and obligations and of any criminal charge against him.

Article 11.

- (1) Everyone charged with a penal offence has the right to be presumed innocent until proved guilty according to law in a public trial at which he has had all the guarantees necessary for his defense.

- (2) No one shall be held guilty of any penal offence on account of any act or omission which did not constitute a penal offence, under national or international law, at the time when it was committed. Nor shall a heavier penalty be imposed than the one that was applicable at the time the penal offence was committed.

Article 12.

- No one shall be subjected to arbitrary interference with his privacy, family, home or correspondence, or to attacks upon his honor and reputation. Everyone has the right to the protection of the law against such interference or attacks.

Article 13.

- (1) Everyone has the right to freedom of movement and residence within the borders of each state.
- (2) Everyone has the right to leave any country, including his own, and to return to his country.

Article 14.

- (1) Everyone has the right to seek and to enjoy in other countries asylum from persecution.

- (2) This right may not be invoked in the case of prosecutions genuinely arising from non-political crimes or from acts contrary to the purposes and principles of the United Nations.

Article 15.

- (1) Everyone has the right to a nationality.
- (2) No one shall be arbitrarily deprived of his nationality nor denied the right to change his nationality.

Article 16.

- (1) Men and women of full age, without any limitation due to race, nationality or religion, have the right to marry and to found a family. They are entitled to equal rights as to marriage, during marriage and at its dissolution.
- (2) Marriage shall be entered into only with the free and full consent of the intending spouses.
- (3) The family is the natural and fundamental group unit of society and is entitled to protection by society and the State.

Article 17.

- (1) Everyone has the right to own property alone as well as in association with others.
- (2) No one shall be arbitrarily deprived of his property.

Article 18.

- Everyone has the right to freedom of thought, conscience and religion; this right includes freedom to change his religion or belief, and freedom, either alone or in community with others and in public or private, to manifest his religion or belief in teaching, practice, worship and observance.

Article 19.

- Everyone has the right to freedom of opinion and expression; this right includes freedom to hold opinions without interference and to seek, receive and impart information and ideas through any media and regardless of frontiers.

Article 20.

- (1) Everyone has the right to freedom of peaceful assembly and association.
- (2) No one may be compelled to belong to an association.

Article 21.

- (1) Everyone has the right to take part in the government of his country, directly or through freely chosen representatives.
- (2) Everyone has the right of equal access to public service in his country.
- (3) The will of the people shall be the basis of the authority of government; this will shall be expressed in periodic and genuine elections which shall be by universal and equal suffrage and shall be held by secret vote or by equivalent free voting procedures.

Article 22.

- Everyone, as a member of society, has the right to social security and is entitled to realization, through national effort and international co-operation and in accordance with the organization and resources of each State, of the economic, social and cultural rights indispensable for his dignity and the free development of his personality.

Article 23.

- (1) Everyone has the right to work, to free choice of employment, to just and favourable conditions of work and to protection against unemployment.
- (2) Everyone, without any discrimination, has the right to equal pay for equal work.
- (3) Everyone who works has the right to just and favourable remuneration ensuring for himself and his family an existence worthy of human dignity, and supplemented, if necessary, by other means of social protection.
- (4) Everyone has the right to form and to join trade unions for the protection of his interests.

Article 24.

- Everyone has the right to rest and leisure, including reasonable limitation of working hours and periodic holidays with pay.

Article 25.

- (1) Everyone has the right to a standard of living adequate for the health and well-being of himself and of his family, including food, clothing, housing and medical care and necessary social services, and the right to security in the event of unemployment, sickness, disability, widowhood, old age or other lack of livelihood in circumstances beyond his control.
- (2) Motherhood and childhood are entitled to special care and assistance. All children, whether born in or out of wedlock, shall enjoy the same social protection.

Article 26.

- (1) Everyone has the right to education. Education shall be free, at least in the elementary and fundamental stages. Elementary education shall be compulsory. Technical and professional education shall be made generally available and higher education shall be equally accessible to all on the basis of merit.

- (2) Education shall be directed to the full development of the human personality and to the strengthening of respect for human rights and fundamental freedoms. It shall promote understanding, tolerance and friendship among all nations, racial or religious groups, and shall further the activities of the United Nations for the maintenance of peace.
- (3) Parents have a prior right to choose the kind of education that shall be given to their children.

Article 27.

- (1) Everyone has the right freely to participate in the cultural life of the community, to enjoy the arts and to share in scientific advancement and its benefits.
- (2) Everyone has the right to the protection of the moral and material interests resulting from any scientific, literary or artistic production of which he is the author.

Article 28.

- Everyone is entitled to a social and international order in which the rights and freedoms set forth in this Declaration can be fully realized.

Article 29.

- (1) Everyone has duties to the community in which alone the free and full development of his personality is possible.
- (2) In the exercise of his rights and freedoms, everyone shall be subject only to such limitations as are determined by law solely for the purpose of securing due recognition and respect for the rights and

freedoms of others and of meeting the just requirements of morality, public order and the general welfare in a democratic society.

- (3) These rights and freedoms may in no case be exercised contrary to the purposes and principles of the United Nations.

Article 30.

- Nothing in this Declaration may be interpreted as implying for any State, group or person any right to engage in any activity or to perform any act aimed at the destruction of any of the rights and freedoms set forth herein.

United Nations Convention against Corruption

Preamble

The States Parties to this Convention,

Concerned about the seriousness of problems and threats posed by corruption to the stability and security of societies, undermining the institutions and values of democracy, ethical values and justice and jeopardizing sustainable development and the rule of law,

Concerned also about the links between corruption and other forms of crime, in particular organized crime and economic crime, including moneylaundering,

Concerned further about cases of corruption that involve vast quantities of assets, which may constitute a substantial proportion of the resources of States, and that threaten the political stability and sustainable development of those States,

Convinced that corruption is no longer a local matter but a transnational phenomenon that affects all societies and economies, making international cooperation to prevent and control it essential, Convinced also that a comprehensive and multidisciplinary approach is required to prevent and combat corruption effectively,

Convinced further that the availability of technical assistance can play an important role in enhancing the ability of States, including by strengthening capacity and by institution-building, to prevent and combat corruption effectively,

Convinced that the illicit acquisition of personal wealth can be particularly damaging to democratic institutions, national economies and the rule of law,

Determined to prevent, detect and deter in a more effective manner international transfers of illicitly acquired assets and to strengthen international cooperation in asset recovery,

Acknowledging the fundamental principles of due process of law in criminal proceedings and in civil or administrative proceedings to adjudicate property rights,

Bearing in mind that the prevention and eradication of corruption is a responsibility of all States and that they must cooperate with one another, with the support and involvement of individuals and groups outside the public sector, such as civil society, non-governmental organizations and community-based organizations, if their efforts in this area are to be effective,

Bearing also in mind the principles of proper management of public affairs and public property, fairness, responsibility and equality before the law and the need to safeguard integrity and to foster a culture of rejection of corruption,

Commending the work of the Commission on Crime Prevention and Criminal Justice and the United Nations Office on Drugs and Crime in preventing and combating corruption,

Recalling the work carried out by other international and regional organizations in this field, including the activities of the African Union, the Council of Europe, the Customs Cooperation Council (also known as the World

Customs Organization), the European Union, the League of Arab States, the Organisation for Economic Cooperation and Development and the Organization of American States,

Taking note with appreciation of multilateral instruments to prevent and combat corruption, including, inter alia, the Inter-American Convention against Corruption, adopted by the Organization of American States on 29 March 1996,[1] the Convention on the Fight against Corruption involving Officials of the European Communities or Officials of Member States of the European Union, adopted by the Council of the European Union on 26 May 1997,[2] the Convention on Combating Bribery of Foreign Public Officials in International Business Transactions, adopted by the Organisation for Economic Cooperation and Development on 21 November 1997,[3] the Criminal Law Convention on Corruption, adopted by the Committee of Ministers of the Council of Europe on 27 January 1999,[4] the Civil Law Convention on Corruption, adopted by the Committee of Ministers of the Council of Europe on 4 November 1999,[5] and the African Union Convention on Preventing and Combating Corruption, adopted by the Heads of State and Government of the African Union on 12 July 2003,

Welcoming the entry into force on 29 September 2003 of the United Nations Convention against Transnational Organized Crime,[6]

Have agreed as follows:

---

[1] See E/1996/99.
[2] Official Journal of the European Communities, C 195, 25 June 1997.
[3] See Corruption and Integrity Improvement Initiatives in Developing Countries (United Nations publication, Sales No. E.98.III.B.18).
[4] Council of Europe, European Treaty Series, No. 173.
[5] Ibid., No. 174.

Chapter I
General provisions

Article 1. Statement of purpose

The purposes of this Convention are:

(*a*) To promote and strengthen measures to prevent and combat corruption more efficiently and effectively;

(*b*) To promote, facilitate and support international cooperation and technical assistance in the prevention of and fight against corruption, including in asset recovery;

(*c*) To promote integrity, accountability and proper management of public affairs and public property.

Article 2. Use of terms

For the purposes of this Convention:

(*a*) "Public official" shall mean: (i) any person holding a legislative, executive, administrative or judicial office of a State Party, whether appointed or elected, whether permanent or temporary, whether paid or unpaid, irrespective of that person's seniority; (ii) any other person who performs a public function, including for a public agency or public enterprise, or provides a public service, as defined in the domestic law of the State Party and as applied in the pertinent area of law of that State Party; (iii) any other person defined as a "public official" in the domestic law of a State Party. However, for the purpose of some specific measures contained in chapter II of this Convention, "public official" may mean any person who performs a public function or provides a public service as defined in the domestic law of the State Party and as applied in the pertinent area of law of that State Party;

(*b*) "Foreign public official" shall mean any person holding a legislative, executive, administrative or judicial

---

⁶General Assembly resolution 55/25, annex I.

office of a foreign country, whether appointed or elected; and any person exercising a public function for a foreign country, including for a public agency or public enterprise;

(c) "Official of a public international organization" shall mean an international civil servant or any person who is authorized by such an organization to act on behalf of that organization;

(d) "Property" shall mean assets of every kind, whether corporeal or incorporeal, movable or immovable, tangible or intangible, and legal documents or instruments evidencing title to or interest in such assets;

(e) "Proceeds of crime" shall mean any property derived from or obtained, directly or indirectly, through the commission of an offence;

(f) "Freezing" or "seizure" shall mean temporarily prohibiting the transfer, conversion, disposition or movement of property or temporarily assuming custody or control of property on the basis of an order issued by a court or other competent authority;

(g) "Confiscation", which includes forfeiture where applicable, shall mean the permanent deprivation of property by order of a court or other competent authority;

(h) "Predicate offence" shall mean any offence as a result of which proceeds have been generated that may become the subject of an offence as defined in article 23 of this Convention;

(i) "Controlled delivery" shall mean the technique of allowing illicit or suspect consignments to pass out of, through or into the territory of one or more States, with the knowledge and under the supervision of their competent authorities, with a view to the investigation of an offence and the identification of persons involved in the commission of the offence.

Article 3. *Scope of application*

1. This Convention shall apply, in accordance with its terms, to the prevention, investigation and prosecution of corruption and to the freezing, seizure, confiscation and return of the proceeds of offences established in accordance with this Convention.

2. For the purposes of implementing this Convention, it shall not be necessary, except as otherwise stated herein, for the offences set forth in it to result in damage or harm to state property.

Article 4. *Protection of sovereignty*

1. States Parties shall carry out their obligations under this Convention in a manner consistent with the principles of sovereign equality and territorial integrity of States and that of non-intervention in the domestic affairs of other States.

2. Nothing in this Convention shall entitle a State Party to undertake in the territory of another State the exercise of jurisdiction and performance of functions that are reserved exclusively for the authorities of that other State by its domestic law.

Chapter II
Preventive measures

Article 5. *Preventive anti-corruption policies and practices*

1. Each State Party shall, in accordance with the fundamental principles of its legal system, develop and implement or maintain effective, coordinated anti-corruption policies that promote the participation of

society and reflect the principles of the rule of law, proper management of public affairs and public property, integrity, transparency and accountability.

2. Each State Party shall endeavour to establish and promote effective practices aimed at the prevention of corruption.

3. Each State Party shall endeavour to periodically evaluate relevant legal instruments and administrative measures with a view to determining their adequacy to prevent and fight corruption.

4. States Parties shall, as appropriate and in accordance with the fundamental principles of their legal system, collaborate with each other and with relevant international and regional organizations in promoting and developing the measures referred to in this article. That collaboration may include participation in international programmes and projects aimed at the prevention of corruption.

Article 6. Preventive anti-corruption body or bodies

1. Each State Party shall, in accordance with the fundamental principles of its legal system, ensure the existence of a body or bodies, as appropriate, that prevent corruption by such means as:

(a) Implementing the policies referred to in article 5 of this Convention
and, where appropriate, overseeing and coordinating the implementation of those policies;

(b) Increasing and disseminating knowledge about the prevention of corruption.

2. Each State Party shall grant the body or bodies referred to in paragraph 1 of this article the necessary independence, in accordance with the fundamental principles of its legal system, to enable the body or bodies to carry out its or their functions effectively and free from

any undue influence. The necessary material resources and specialized staff, as well as the training that such staff may require to carry out their functions, should be provided.

3. Each State Party shall inform the Secretary-General of the United Nations of the name and address of the authority or authorities that may assist other States Parties in developing and implementing specific measures for the prevention of corruption.

Article 7. *Public sector*

1. Each State Party shall, where appropriate and in accordance with the fundamental principles of its legal system, endeavour to adopt, maintain and strengthen systems for the recruitment, hiring, retention, promotion and retirement of civil servants and, where appropriate, other non-elected public officials:

(*a*) That are based on principles of efficiency, transparency and objective criteria such as merit, equity and aptitude;

(*b*) That include adequate procedures for the selection and training of individuals for public positions considered especially vulnerable to corruption and the rotation, where appropriate, of such individuals to other positions;

(*c*) That promote adequate remuneration and equitable pay scales, taking into account the level of economic development of the State Party;

(*d*) That promote education and training programmes to enable them to meet the requirements for the correct, honourable and proper performance of public functions and that provide them with specialized and appropriate training to enhance their awareness of the risks of corruption inherent in the performance of their functions. Such programmes may make reference to codes or standards of conduct in applicable areas.

2. Each State Party shall also consider adopting appropriate legislative and administrative measures, consistent with the objectives of this Convention and in accordance with the fundamental principles of its domestic law, to prescribe criteria concerning candidature for and election to public office.

3. Each State Party shall also consider taking appropriate legislative and administrative measures, consistent with the objectives of this Convention and in accordance with the fundamental principles of its domestic law, to enhance transparency in the funding of candidatures for elected public office and, where applicable, the funding of political parties.

4. Each State Party shall, in accordance with the fundamental principles of its domestic law, endeavour to adopt, maintain and strengthen systems that promote transparency and prevent conflicts of interest.

Article 8. Codes of conduct for public officials

1. In order to fight corruption, each State Party shall promote, inter alia, integrity, honesty and responsibility among its public officials, in accordance with the fundamental principles of its legal system.

2. In particular, each State Party shall endeavour to apply, within its own institutional and legal systems, codes or standards of conduct for the correct, honourable and proper performance of public functions.

3. For the purposes of implementing the provisions of this article, each State Party shall, where appropriate and in accordance with the fundamental principles of its legal system, take note of the relevant initiatives of regional, interregional and multilateral organizations, such as the International Code of Conduct for Public Officials

contained in the annex to General Assembly resolution 51/59 of 12 December 1996.

4. Each State Party shall also consider, in accordance with the fundamental principles of its domestic law, establishing measures and systems to facilitate the reporting by public officials of acts of corruption to appropriate authorities, when such acts come to their notice in the performance of their functions.

5. Each State Party shall endeavour, where appropriate and in accordance with the fundamental principles of its domestic law, to establish measures and systems requiring public officials to make declarations to appropriate authorities regarding, inter alia, their outside activities, employment, investments, assets and substantial gifts or benefits from which a conflict of interest may result with respect to their functions as public officials.

6. Each State Party shall consider taking, in accordance with the fundamental principles of its domestic law, disciplinary or other measures against public officials who violate the codes or standards established in accordance with this article.

Article 9. Public procurement and management of public finances

1. Each State Party shall, in accordance with the fundamental principles of its legal system, take the necessary steps to establish appropriate systems of procurement, based on transparency, competition and objective criteria in decision-making, that are effective, inter alia, in preventing corruption. Such systems, which may take into account appropriate threshold values in their application, shall address, inter alia:

(*a*) The public distribution of information relating to procurement procedures and contracts, including information on invitations to tender and relevant or pertinent information on the award of contracts, allowing potential tenderers sufficient time to prepare and submit their tenders;

(*b*) The establishment, in advance, of conditions for participation, including selection and award criteria and tendering rules, and their publication;

(*c*) The use of objective and predetermined criteria for public procurement decisions, in order to facilitate the subsequent verification of the correct application of the rules or procedures;

(*d*) An effective system of domestic review, including an effective system of appeal, to ensure legal recourse and remedies in the event that the rules or procedures established pursuant to this paragraph are not followed;

(*e*) Where appropriate, measures to regulate matters regarding personnel responsible for procurement, such as declaration of interest in particular public procurements, screening procedures and training requirements.

2. Each State Party shall, in accordance with the fundamental principles of its legal system, take appropriate measures to promote transparency and accountability in the management of public finances. Such measures shall encompass, inter alia:

(*a*) Procedures for the adoption of the national budget;

(*b*) Timely reporting on revenue and expenditure;

(*c*) A system of accounting and auditing standards and related oversight;

(*d*) Effective and efficient systems of risk management and internal control; and

(*e*) Where appropriate, corrective action in the case of failure to comply with the requirements established in this paragraph.

3. Each State Party shall take such civil and administrative measures as may be necessary, in

accordance with the fundamental principles of its domestic law, to preserve the integrity of accounting books, records, financial statements or other documents related to public expenditure and revenue and to prevent the falsification of such documents.

Article 10. Public reporting
Taking into account the need to combat corruption, each State Party shall, in accordance with the fundamental principles of its domestic law, take such measures as may be necessary to enhance transparency in its public administration, including with regard to its organization, functioning and decisionmaking processes, where appropriate. Such measures may include, inter alia:

(*a*) Adopting procedures or regulations allowing members of the general public to obtain, where appropriate, information on the organization, functioning and decision-making processes of its public administration and, with due regard for the protection of privacy and personal data, on decisions and legal acts that concern members of the public;

(*b*) Simplifying administrative procedures, where appropriate, in order to facilitate public access to the competent decision-making authorities; and

(*c*) Publishing information, which may include periodic reports on the risks of corruption in its public administration.

Article 11. Measures relating to the judiciary and prosecution services

1. Bearing in mind the independence of the judiciary and its crucial role in combating corruption, each State Party shall, in accordance with the fundamental principles of its legal system and without prejudice to judicial independence, take measures to strengthen integrity and to prevent opportunities for corruption among members

of the judiciary. Such measures may include rules with respect to the conduct of members of the judiciary.

2. Measures to the same effect as those taken pursuant to paragraph 1 of this article may be introduced and applied within the prosecution service in those States Parties where it does not form part of the judiciary but enjoys independence similar to that of the judicial service.

Article 12. *Private sector*

1. Each State Party shall take measures, in accordance with the fundamental principles of its domestic law, to prevent corruption involving the private sector, enhance accounting and auditing standards in the private sector and, where appropriate, provide effective, proportionate and dissuasive civil, administrative or criminal penalties for failure to comply with such measures.

2. Measures to achieve these ends may include, inter alia:

(*a*) Promoting cooperation between law enforcement agencies and relevant private entities;

(*b*) Promoting the development of standards and procedures designed to safeguard the integrity of relevant private entities, including codes of conduct for the correct, honourable and proper performance of the activities of business and all relevant professions and the prevention of conflicts of interest, and for the promotion of the use of good commercial practices among businesses and in the contractual relations of businesses with the State;

(*c*) Promoting transparency among private entities, including, where appropriate, measures regarding the identity of legal and natural persons involved in the establishment and management of corporate entities;

(*d*) Preventing the misuse of procedures regulating private entities, including procedures regarding subsidies and licences granted by public authorities for commercial activities;

(*e*) Preventing conflicts of interest by imposing restrictions, as appropriate and for a reasonable period of time, on the professional activities of former public officials or on the employment of public officials by the private sector after their resignation or retirement, where such activities or employment relate directly to the functions held or supervised by those public officials during their tenure;

(*f*) Ensuring that private enterprises, taking into account their structure and size, have sufficient internal auditing controls to assist in preventing and detecting acts of corruption and that the accounts and required financial statements of such private enterprises are subject to appropriate auditing and certification procedures.

3. In order to prevent corruption, each State Party shall take such measures as may be necessary, in accordance with its domestic laws and regulations regarding the maintenance of books and records, financial statement disclosures and accounting and auditing standards, to prohibit the following acts carried out for the purpose of committing any of the offences established in accordance with this Convention:

(*a*) The establishment of off-the-books accounts;

(*b*) The making of off-the-books or inadequately identified transactions;

(*c*) The recording of non-existent expenditure;

(*d*) The entry of liabilities with incorrect identification of their objects;

(*e*) The use of false documents; and

(*f*) The intentional destruction of bookkeeping documents earlier than foreseen by the law.

4. Each State Party shall disallow the tax deductibility of expenses that constitute bribes, the latter being one of the constituent elements of the offences established in accordance with articles 15 and 16 of this Convention and,

where appropriate, other expenses incurred in furtherance of corrupt conduct.

Article 13. *Participation of society*

1. Each State Party shall take appropriate measures, within its means and in accordance with fundamental principles of its domestic law, to promote the active participation of individuals and groups outside the public sector, such as civil society, non-governmental organizations and community-based organizations, in the prevention of and the fight against corruption and to raise public awareness regarding the existence, causes and gravity of and the threat posed by corruption. This participation should be strengthened by such measures as:

(*a*) Enhancing the transparency of and promoting the contribution of the public to decision-making processes;

(*b*) Ensuring that the public has effective access to information;

(*c*) Undertaking public information activities that contribute to nontolerance of corruption, as well as public education programmes, including school and university curricula;

(*d*) Respecting, promoting and protecting the freedom to seek, receive, publish and disseminate information concerning corruption. That freedom may be subject to certain restrictions, but these shall only be such as are provided for by law and are necessary:

(*i*) For respect of the rights or reputations of others;

(*ii*) For the protection of national security or ordre public or of public health or morals.

2. Each State Party shall take appropriate measures to ensure that the relevant anti-corruption bodies referred to in this Convention are known to the public and shall provide access to such bodies, where appropriate, for the reporting, including anonymously, of any incidents that

may be considered to constitute an offence established in accordance with this Convention.

Article 14. Measures to prevent money-laundering

1. Each State Party shall:

(*a*) Institute a comprehensive domestic regulatory and supervisory regime for banks and non-bank financial institutions, including natural or legal persons that provide formal or informal services for the transmission of money or value and, where appropriate, other bodies particularly susceptible to moneylaundering, within its competence, in order to deter and detect all forms of money-laundering, which regime shall emphasize requirements for customer and, where appropriate, beneficial owner identification, record-keeping and the reporting of suspicious transactions;

(*b*) Without prejudice to article 46 of this Convention, ensure that administrative, regulatory, law enforcement and other authorities dedicated to combating money-laundering (including, where appropriate under domestic law, judicial authorities) have the ability to cooperate and exchange information at the national and international levels within the conditions prescribed by its domestic law and, to that end, shall consider the establishment of a financial intelligence unit to serve as a national centre for the collection, analysis and dissemination of information regarding potential money-laundering.

2. States Parties shall consider implementing feasible measures to detect and monitor the movement of cash and appropriate negotiable instruments across their borders, subject to safeguards to ensure proper use of information and without impeding in any way the movement of legitimate capital. Such measures may include a requirement that individuals and businesses report the cross-border transfer of substantial quantities of cash and appropriate negotiable instruments.

3. States Parties shall consider implementing appropriate and feasible measures to require financial institutions, including money remitters:

(a) To include on forms for the electronic transfer of funds and related messages accurate and meaningful information on the originator;

(b) To maintain such information throughout the payment chain; and

(c) To apply enhanced scrutiny to transfers of funds that do not contain complete information on the originator.

4. In establishing a domestic regulatory and supervisory regime under the terms of this article, and without prejudice to any other article of this Convention, States Parties are called upon to use as a guideline the relevant initiatives of regional, interregional and multilateral organizations against money-laundering.

5. States Parties shall endeavour to develop and promote global, regional, subregional and bilateral cooperation among judicial, law enforcement and financial regulatory authorities in order to combat money-laundering.

Chapter III
Criminalization and law enforcement

Article 15. Bribery of national public officials

Each State Party shall adopt such legislative and other measures as may be necessary to establish as criminal offences, when committed intentionally:

(a) The promise, offering or giving, to a public official, directly or indirectly, of an undue advantage, for the official himself or herself or another person or entity, in order that the official act or refrain from acting in the exercise of his or her official duties;

(b) The solicitation or acceptance by a public official, directly or indirectly, of an undue advantage, for the official himself or herself or another person or entity, in order that the official act or refrain from acting in the exercise of his or her official duties.

Article 16. *Bribery of foreign public officials and officials of public international organizations*

1. Each State Party shall adopt such legislative and other measures as may be necessary to establish as a criminal offence, when committed intentionally, the promise, offering or giving to a foreign public official or an official of a public international organization, directly or indirectly, of an undue advantage, for the official himself or herself or another person or entity, in order that the official act or refrain from acting in the exercise of his or her official duties, in order to obtain or retain business or other undue advantage in relation to the conduct of international business.

2. Each State Party shall consider adopting such legislative and other measures as may be necessary to establish as a criminal offence, when committed intentionally, the solicitation or acceptance by a foreign public official or an official of a public international organization, directly or indirectly, of an undue advantage, for the official himself or herself or another person or entity, in order that the official act or refrain from acting in the exercise of his or her official duties.

Article 17. *Embezzlement, misappropriation or other diversion of property by a public official*

Each State Party shall adopt such legislative and other measures as may be necessary to establish as criminal offences, when committed intentionally, the embezzlement, misappropriation or other diversion by a public official for his or her benefit or for the benefit of another person or entity, of any property, public or private funds or securities or any other thing of value entrusted to the public official by virtue of his or her position.

Article 18. *Trading in influence*

Each State Party shall consider adopting such legislative and other measures as may be necessary to establish as criminal offences, when committed intentionally:

(*a*) The promise, offering or giving to a public official or any other person, directly or indirectly, of an undue advantage in order that the public official or the person abuse his or her real or supposed influence with a view to obtaining from an administration or public authority of the State Party an undue advantage for the original instigator of the act or for any other person;

(*b*) The solicitation or acceptance by a public official or any other person, directly or indirectly, of an undue advantage for himself or herself or for another person in order that the public official or the person abuse his or her real or supposed influence with a view to obtaining from an administration or public authority of the State Party an undue advantage.

Article 19. *Abuse of functions*

Each State Party shall consider adopting such legislative and other measures as may be necessary to establish as a criminal offence, when committed intentionally, the abuse of functions or position, that is, the performance of or failure to perform an act, in violation of laws, by a public official in the discharge of his or her functions, for the purpose of obtaining an undue advantage for himself or herself or for another person or entity.

Article 20. *Illicit enrichment*

Subject to its constitution and the fundamental principles of its legal system, each State Party shall consider adopting such legislative and other measures as may be necessary to establish as a criminal offence, when committed intentionally, illicit enrichment, that is, a significant increase in the assets of a public official that he or she cannot reasonably explain in relation to his or her lawful income.

Article 21. *Bribery in the private sector*

Each State Party shall consider adopting such legislative and other measures as may be necessary to establish as criminal offences, when committed intentionally in the course of economic, financial or commercial activities:

(a) The promise, offering or giving, directly or indirectly, of an undue advantage to any person who directs or works, in any capacity, for a private sector entity, for the person himself or herself or for another person, in order that he or she, in breach of his or her duties, act or refrain from acting;

(b) The solicitation or acceptance, directly or indirectly, of an undue advantage by any person who directs or works, in any capacity, for a private sector entity, for the person himself or herself or for another person, in order that he or she, in breach of his or her duties, act or refrain from acting.

Article 22. Embezzlement of property in the private sector

Each State Party shall consider adopting such legislative and other measures as may be necessary to establish as a criminal offence, when committed intentionally in the course of economic, financial or commercial activities, embezzlement by a person who directs or works, in any capacity, in a private sector entity of any property, private funds or securities or any other thing of value entrusted to him or her by virtue of his or her position.

Article 23. Laundering of proceeds of crime

1. Each State Party shall adopt, in accordance with fundamental principles of its domestic law, such legislative and other measures as may be necessary to establish as criminal offences, when committed intentionally:

(*a*) (i) The conversion or transfer of property, knowing that such property is the proceeds of crime, for the purpose of concealing or disguising the illicit origin of the property or of helping any person who is involved in the commission of the predicate offence to evade the legal consequences of his or her action; (ii) The concealment or disguise of the true nature, source, location, disposition, movement or ownership of or rights with respect to property, knowing that such property is the proceeds of crime;

(*b*) Subject to the basic concepts of its legal system: (i) The acquisition, possession or use of property, knowing, at the time of receipt, that such property is the proceeds of crime; (ii) Participation in, association with or conspiracy to commit, attempts to commit and aiding, abetting, facilitating and counselling the commission of any of the offences established in accordance with this article.

2. For purposes of implementing or applying paragraph 1 of this article:

(a) Each State Party shall seek to apply paragraph 1 of this article to the widest range of predicate offences;

(b) Each State Party shall include as predicate offences at a minimum a comprehensive range of criminal offences established in accordance with this Convention;

(c) For the purposes of subparagraph (b) above, predicate offences shall include offences committed both within and outside the jurisdiction of the State Party in question. However, offences committed outside the jurisdiction of a State Party shall constitute predicate offences only when the relevant conduct is a criminal offence under the domestic law of the State where it is committed and would be a criminal offence under the domestic law of the State Party implementing or applying this article had it been committed there;

(d) Each State Party shall furnish copies of its laws that give effect to this article and of any subsequent changes to such laws or a description thereof to the Secretary-General of the United Nations;

(e) If required by fundamental principles of the domestic law of a State Party, it may be provided that the offences set forth in paragraph 1 of this article do not apply to the persons who committed the predicate offence.

Article 24. Concealment

Without prejudice to the provisions of article 23 of this Convention, each State Party shall consider adopting such legislative and other measures as may be necessary to establish as a criminal offence, when committed intentionally after the commission of any of the offences established in accordance with this Convention without having participated in such offences, the concealment or continued retention of property when the person involved knows that such property is the result of any of the offences established in accordance with this Convention.

Article 25. *Obstruction of justice*

Each State Party shall adopt such legislative and other measures as may be necessary to establish as criminal offences, when committed intentionally:

(a) The use of physical force, threats or intimidation or the promise, offering or giving of an undue advantage to induce false testimony or to interfere in the giving of testimony or the production of evidence in a proceeding in relation to the commission of offences established in accordance with this Convention;

(b) The use of physical force, threats or intimidation to interfere with the exercise of official duties by a justice or law enforcement official in relation to the commission of offences established in accordance with this Convention. Nothing in this subparagraph shall prejudice the right of States Parties to have legislation that protects other categories of public official.

Article 26. *Liability of legal persons*

1. Each State Party shall adopt such measures as may be necessary, consistent with its legal principles, to establish the liability of legal persons for participation in the offences established in accordance with this Convention.

2. Subject to the legal principles of the State Party, the liability of legal persons may be criminal, civil or administrative.

3. Such liability shall be without prejudice to the criminal liability of the natural persons who have committed the offences.

4. Each State Party shall, in particular, ensure that legal persons held liable in accordance with this article are subject to effective, proportionate and dissuasive criminal or non-criminal sanctions, including monetary sanctions.

Article 27. Participation and attempt

1. Each State Party shall adopt such legislative and other measures as may be necessary to establish as a criminal offence, in accordance with its domestic law, participation in any capacity such as an accomplice, assistant or instigator in an offence established in accordance with this Convention.

2. Each State Party may adopt such legislative and other measures as may be necessary to establish as a criminal offence, in accordance with its domestic law, any attempt to commit an offence established in accordance with this Convention.

3. Each State Party may adopt such legislative and other measures as may be necessary to establish as a criminal offence, in accordance with its domestic law, the preparation for an offence established in accordance with this Convention.

Article 28. Knowledge, intent and purpose as elements of an offence

Knowledge, intent or purpose required as an element of an offence established in accordance with this Convention may be inferred from objective factual circumstances.

Article 29. Statute of limitations

Each State Party shall, where appropriate, establish under its domestic law a long statute of limitations period in which to commence proceedings for any offence established in accordance with this Convention and establish a longer statute of limitations period or provide for the suspension of the statute of limitations where the alleged offender has evaded the administration of justice.

Article 30. *Prosecution, adjudication and sanctions*

1. Each State Party shall make the commission of an offence established in accordance with this Convention liable to sanctions that take into account the gravity of that offence.

2. Each State Party shall take such measures as may be necessary to establish or maintain, in accordance with its legal system and constitutional principles, an appropriate balance between any immunities or jurisdictional privileges accorded to its public officials for the performance of their functions and the possibility, when necessary, of effectively investigating, prosecuting and adjudicating offences established in accordance with this Convention.

3. Each State Party shall endeavour to ensure that any discretionary legal powers under its domestic law relating to the prosecution of persons for offences established in accordance with this Convention are exercised to maximize the effectiveness of law enforcement measures in respect of those offences and with due regard to the need to deter the commission of such offences.

4. In the case of offences established in accordance with this Convention, each State Party shall take appropriate measures, in accordance with its domestic law and with due regard to the rights of the defence, to seek to ensure that conditions imposed in connection with decisions on release pending trial or appeal take into consideration the need to ensure the presence of the defendant at subsequent criminal proceedings.

5. Each State Party shall take into account the gravity of the offences concerned when considering the eventuality of early release or parole of persons convicted of such offences.

6. Each State Party, to the extent consistent with the fundamental principles of its legal system, shall consider establishing procedures through which a public official accused of an offence established in accordance with this Convention may, where appropriate, be removed, suspended or reassigned by the appropriate authority, bearing in mind respect for the principle of the presumption of innocence.

7. Where warranted by the gravity of the offence, each State Party, to the extent consistent with the fundamental principles of its legal system, shall consider establishing procedures for the disqualification, by court order or any other appropriate means, for a period of time determined by its domestic law, of persons convicted of offences established in accordance with this Convention from:

(a) Holding public office; and

(b) Holding office in an enterprise owned in whole or in part by the State.

8. Paragraph 1 of this article shall be without prejudice to the exercise of disciplinary powers by the competent authorities against civil servants.

9. Nothing contained in this Convention shall affect the principle that the description of the offences established in accordance with this Convention and of the applicable legal defences or other legal principles controlling the lawfulness of conduct is reserved to the domestic law of a State Party and that such offences shall be prosecuted and punished in accordance with that law.

10. States Parties shall endeavour to promote the reintegration into society of persons convicted of offences established in accordance with this Convention.

Article 31. *Freezing, seizure and confiscation*

1. Each State Party shall take, to the greatest extent possible within its domestic legal system, such measures as may be necessary to enable confiscation of:

(*a*) Proceeds of crime derived from offences established in accordance with this Convention or property the value of which corresponds to that of such proceeds;

(*b*) Property, equipment or other instrumentalities used in or destined for use in offences established in accordance with this Convention.

2. Each State Party shall take such measures as may be necessary to enable the identification, tracing, freezing or seizure of any item referred to in paragraph 1 of this article for the purpose of eventual confiscation.

3. Each State Party shall adopt, in accordance with its domestic law, such legislative and other measures as may be necessary to regulate the administration by the competent authorities of frozen, seized or confiscated property covered in paragraphs 1 and 2 of this article.

4. If such proceeds of crime have been transformed or converted, in part or in full, into other property, such property shall be liable to the measures referred to in this article instead of the proceeds.

5. If such proceeds of crime have been intermingled with property acquired from legitimate sources, such property shall, without prejudice to any powers relating to freezing or seizure, be liable to confiscation up to the assessed value of the intermingled proceeds.

6. Income or other benefits derived from such proceeds of crime, from property into which such proceeds of crime have been transformed or converted or from property with which such proceeds of crime have been intermingled shall also be liable to the measures referred to in this article, in the same manner and to the same extent as proceeds of crime.

7. For the purpose of this article and article 55 of this Convention, each State Party shall empower its courts or other competent authorities to order that bank, financial or commercial records be made available or seized. A State Party shall not decline to act under the provisions of this paragraph on the ground of bank secrecy.

8. States Parties may consider the possibility of requiring that an offender demonstrate the lawful origin of such alleged proceeds of crime or other property liable to confiscation, to the extent that such a requirement is consistent with the fundamental principles of their domestic law and with the nature of judicial and other proceedings.

9. The provisions of this article shall not be so construed as to prejudice the rights of bona fide third parties.

10. Nothing contained in this article shall affect the principle that the measures to which it refers shall be defined and implemented in accordance with and subject to the provisions of the domestic law of a State Party.

Article 32. Protection of witnesses, experts and victims

1. Each State Party shall take appropriate measures in accordance with its domestic legal system and within its means to provide effective protection from potential retaliation or intimidation for witnesses and experts who give testimony concerning offences established in

accordance with this Convention and, as appropriate, for their relatives and other persons close to them.

2. The measures envisaged in paragraph 1 of this article may include, inter alia, without prejudice to the rights of the defendant, including the right to due process:

(a) Establishing procedures for the physical protection of such persons, such as, to the extent necessary and feasible, relocating them and permitting, where appropriate, non-disclosure or limitations on the disclosure of information concerning the identity and whereabouts of such persons;

(b) Providing evidentiary rules to permit witnesses and experts to give testimony in a manner that ensures the safety of such persons, such as permitting testimony to be given through the use of communications technology such as video or other adequate means.

3. States Parties shall consider entering into agreements or arrangements with other States for the relocation of persons referred to in paragraph 1 of this article.

4. The provisions of this article shall also apply to victims insofar as they are witnesses.

5. Each State Party shall, subject to its domestic law, enable the views and concerns of victims to be presented and considered at appropriate stages of criminal proceedings against offenders in a manner not prejudicial to the rights of the defence.

Article 33. Protection of reporting persons

Each State Party shall consider incorporating into its domestic legal system appropriate measures to provide protection against any unjustified treatment for any person who reports in good faith and on reasonable grounds to the competent authorities any facts concerning offences established in accordance with this Convention.

Article 34. Consequences of acts of corruption
With due regard to the rights of third parties acquired in good faith, each State Party shall take measures, in accordance with the fundamental principles of its domestic law, to address consequences of corruption. In this context, States Parties may consider corruption a relevant factor in legal proceedings to annul or rescind a contract, withdraw a concession or other similar instrument or take any other remedial action.

Article 35. Compensation for damage

Each State Party shall take such measures as may be necessary, in accordance with principles of its domestic law, to ensure that entities or persons who have suffered damage as a result of an act of corruption have the right to initiate legal proceedings against those responsible for that damage in order to obtain compensation.

Article 36. Specialized authorities

Each State Party shall, in accordance with the fundamental principles of its legal system, ensure the existence of a body or bodies or persons specialized in combating corruption through law enforcement. Such body or bodies or persons shall be granted the necessary independence, in accordance with the fundamental principles of the legal system of the State Party, to be able to carry out their functions effectively and without any undue influence. Such persons or staff of such body or bodies should have the appropriate training and resources to carry out their tasks.

Article 37. Cooperation with law enforcement authorities

1. Each State Party shall take appropriate measures to encourage persons who participate or who have participated in the commission of an offence established in

accordance with this Convention to supply information useful to competent authorities for investigative and evidentiary purposes and to provide factual, specific help to competent authorities that may contribute to depriving offenders of the proceeds of crime and to recovering such proceeds.

2. Each State Party shall consider providing for the possibility, in appropriate cases, of mitigating punishment of an accused person who provides substantial cooperation in the investigation or prosecution of an offence established in accordance with this Convention.

3. Each State Party shall consider providing for the possibility, in accordance with fundamental principles of its domestic law, of granting immunity from prosecution to a person who provides substantial cooperation in the investigation or prosecution of an offence established in accordance with this Convention.

4. Protection of such persons shall be, mutatis mutandis, as provided for in article 32 of this Convention. 5. Where a person referred to in paragraph 1 of this article located in one State Party can provide substantial cooperation to the competent authorities of another State Party, the States Parties concerned may consider entering into agreements or arrangements, in accordance with their domestic law, concerning the potential provision by the other State Party of the treatment set forth in paragraphs 2 and 3 of this article.

Article 38. *Cooperation between national authorities*

Each State Party shall take such measures as may be necessary to encourage, in accordance with its domestic law, cooperation between, on the one hand, its public authorities, as well as its public officials, and, on the other hand, its authorities responsible for investigating and prosecuting criminal offences. Such cooperation may include:

(a) Informing the latter authorities, on their own initiative, where there are reasonable grounds to believe that any of the offences established in accordance with articles 15, 21 and 23 of this Convention has been committed; or

(b) Providing, upon request, to the latter authorities all necessary information.

Article 39. Cooperation between national authorities and the private sector

1. Each State Party shall take such measures as may be necessary to encourage, in accordance with its domestic law, cooperation between national investigating and prosecuting authorities and entities of the private sector, in particular financial institutions, relating to matters involving the commission of offences established in accordance with this Convention.

2. Each State Party shall consider encouraging its nationals and other persons with a habitual residence in its territory to report to the national investigating and prosecuting authorities the commission of an offence established in accordance with this Convention.

Article 40. Bank secrecy

Each State Party shall ensure that, in the case of domestic criminal investigations of offences established in accordance with this Convention, there are appropriate mechanisms available within its domestic legal system to overcome obstacles that may arise out of the application of bank secrecy laws.

Article 41. Criminal record

Each State Party may adopt such legislative or other

measures as may be necessary to take into consideration, under such terms as and for the purpose that it deems appropriate, any previous conviction in another State of an alleged offender for the purpose of using such information in criminal proceedings relating to an offence established in accordance with this Convention.

Article 42. *Jurisdiction*

1. Each State Party shall adopt such measures as may be necessary to establish its jurisdiction over the offences established in accordance with this Convention when:

(*a*) The offence is committed in the territory of that State Party; or

(*b*) The offence is committed on board a vessel that is flying the flag of that State Party or an aircraft that is registered under the laws of that State Party at the time that the offence is committed.

2. Subject to article 4 of this Convention, a State Party may also establish its jurisdiction over any such offence when:

(*a*) The offence is committed against a national of that State Party; or

(*b*) The offence is committed by a national of that State Party or a stateless person who has his or her habitual residence in its territory; or

(*c*) The offence is one of those established in accordance with article 23, paragraph 1 (b) (ii), of this Convention and is committed outside its territory with a view to the commission of an offence established in accordance with article 23, paragraph 1 (a) (i) or (ii) or (b) (i), of this Convention within its territory; or (d) The offence is committed against the State Party.

3. For the purposes of article 44 of this Convention, each State Party shall take such measures as may be necessary to establish its jurisdiction over the offences

established in accordance with this Convention when the alleged offender is present in its territory and it does not extradite such person solely on the ground that he or she is one of its nationals.

4. Each State Party may also take such measures as may be necessary to establish its jurisdiction over the offences established in accordance with this Convention when the alleged offender is present in its territory and it does not extradite him or her.

5. If a State Party exercising its jurisdiction under paragraph 1 or 2 of this article has been notified, or has otherwise learned, that any other States Parties are conducting an investigation, prosecution or judicial proceeding in respect of the same conduct, the competent authorities of those States Parties shall, as appropriate, consult one another with a view to coordinating their actions.

6. Without prejudice to norms of general international law, this Convention shall not exclude the exercise of any criminal jurisdiction established by a State Party in accordance with its domestic law.

Chapter IV
International cooperation

Article 43. International cooperation

1. States Parties shall cooperate in criminal matters in accordance with articles 44 to 50 of this Convention. Where appropriate and consistent with their domestic legal system, States Parties shall consider assisting each other in investigations of and proceedings in civil and administrative matters relating to corruption.

2. In matters of international cooperation, whenever dual criminality is considered a requirement, it shall be deemed fulfilled irrespective of whether the laws of the requested State Party place the offence within the same category of offence or denominate the offence by the same terminology as the requesting State Party, if the conduct underlying the offence for which assistance is sought is a criminal offence under the laws of both States Parties.

Article 44. Extradition

1. This article shall apply to the offences established in accordance with this Convention where the person who is the subject of the request for extradition is present in the territory of the requested State Party, provided that the offence for which extradition is sought is punishable under the domestic law of both the requesting State Party and the requested State Party.

2. Notwithstanding the provisions of paragraph 1 of this article, a State Party whose law so permits may grant the extradition of a person for any of the offences covered by this Convention that are not punishable under its own domestic law.

3. If the request for extradition includes several separate offences, at least one of which is extraditable under this article and some of which are not extraditable by reason of their period of imprisonment but are related to offences established in accordance with this Convention, the requested State Party may apply this article also in respect of those offences.

4. Each of the offences to which this article applies shall be deemed to be included as an extraditable offence in any extradition treaty existing between States Parties. States Parties undertake to include such offences as extraditable offences in every extradition treaty to be concluded

between them. A State Party whose law so permits, in case it uses this Convention as the basis for extradition, shall not consider any of the offences established in accordance with this Convention to be a political offence.

5. If a State Party that makes extradition conditional on the existence of a treaty receives a request for extradition from another State Party with which it has no extradition treaty, it may consider this Convention the legal basis for extradition in respect of any offence to which this article applies.

6. A State Party that makes extradition conditional on the existence of a treaty shall:

(a) At the time of deposit of its instrument of ratification, acceptance or approval of or accession to this Convention, inform the Secretary-General of the United Nations whether it will take this Convention as the legal basis for cooperation on extradition with other States Parties to this Convention; and

(b) If it does not take this Convention as the legal basis for cooperation on extradition, seek, where appropriate, to conclude treaties on extradition with other States Parties to this Convention in order to implement this article.

7. States Parties that do not make extradition conditional on the existence of a treaty shall recognize offences to which this article applies as extraditable offences between themselves.

8. Extradition shall be subject to the conditions provided for by the domestic law of the requested State Party or by applicable extradition treaties, including, inter alia, conditions in relation to the minimum penalty requirement for extradition and the grounds upon which the requested State Party may refuse extradition.

9. States Parties shall, subject to their domestic law, endeavour to expedite extradition procedures and to

simplify evidentiary requirements relating thereto in respect of any offence to which this article applies.

10. Subject to the provisions of its domestic law and its extradition treaties, the requested State Party may, upon being satisfied that the circumstances so warrant and are urgent and at the request of the requesting State Party, take a person whose extradition is sought and who is present in its territory into custody or take other appropriate measures to ensure his or her presence at extradition proceedings.

11. A State Party in whose territory an alleged offender is found, if it does not extradite such person in respect of an offence to which this article applies solely on the ground that he or she is one of its nationals, shall, at the request of the State Party seeking extradition, be obliged to submit the case without undue delay to its competent authorities for the purpose of prosecution. Those authorities shall take their decision and conduct their proceedings in the same manner as in the case of any other offence of a grave nature under the domestic law of that State Party. The States Parties concerned shall cooperate with each other, in particular on procedural and evidentiary aspects, to ensure the efficiency of such prosecution.

12. Whenever a State Party is permitted under its domestic law to extradite or otherwise surrender one of its nationals only upon the condition that the person will be returned to that State Party to serve the sentence imposed as a result of the trial or proceedings for which the extradition or surrender of the person was sought and that State Party and the State Party seeking the extradition of the person agree with this option and other terms that they may deem appropriate, such conditional extradition or surrender shall be sufficient to discharge the obligation set forth in paragraph 11 of this article.

13. If extradition, sought for purposes of enforcing a sentence, is refused because the person sought is a national of the requested State Party, the requested State Party shall, if its domestic law so permits and in conformity with the requirements of such law, upon application of the requesting State Party, consider the enforcement of the sentence imposed under the domestic law of the requesting State Party or the remainder thereof.

14. Any person regarding whom proceedings are being carried out in connection with any of the offences to which this article applies shall be guaranteed fair treatment at all stages of the proceedings, including enjoyment of all the rights and guarantees provided by the domestic law of the State Party in the territory of which that person is present.

15. Nothing in this Convention shall be interpreted as imposing an obligation to extradite if the requested State Party has substantial grounds for believing that the request has been made for the purpose of prosecuting or punishing a person on account of that person's sex, race, religion, nationality, ethnic origin or political opinions or that compliance with the request would cause prejudice to that person's position for any one of these reasons.

16. States Parties may not refuse a request for extradition on the sole ground that the offence is also considered to involve fiscal matters.

17. Before refusing extradition, the requested State Party shall, where appropriate, consult with the requesting State Party to provide it with ample opportunity to present its opinions and to provide information relevant to its allegation.

18. States Parties shall seek to conclude bilateral and multilateral agreements or arrangements to carry out or to enhance the effectiveness of extradition.

Article 45. *Transfer of sentenced persons*

States Parties may consider entering into bilateral or multilateral agreements or arrangements on the transfer to their territory of persons sentenced to imprisonment or other forms of deprivation of liberty for offences established in accordance with this Convention in order that they may complete their sentences there.

Article 46. *Mutual legal assistance*

1. States Parties shall afford one another the widest measure of mutual legal assistance in investigations, prosecutions and judicial proceedings in relation to the offences covered by this Convention.

2. Mutual legal assistance shall be afforded to the fullest extent possible under relevant laws, treaties, agreements and arrangements of the requested State Party with respect to investigations, prosecutions and judicial proceedings in relation to the offences for which a legal person may be held liable in accordance with article 26 of this Convention in the requesting State Party.

3. Mutual legal assistance to be afforded in accordance with this article may be requested for any of the following purposes:

(a) Taking evidence or statements from persons;

(b) Effecting service of judicial documents;

(c) Executing searches and seizures, and freezing;

(d) Examining objects and sites;

(e) Providing information, evidentiary items and expert evaluations;

(f) Providing originals or certified copies of relevant documents and records, including government, bank, financial, corporate or business records;

(g) Identifying or tracing proceeds of crime, property, instrumentalities or other things for evidentiary purposes;

(*h*) Facilitating the voluntary appearance of persons in the requesting State Party;

(*i*) Any other type of assistance that is not contrary to the domestic law of the requested State Party;

(*j*) Identifying, freezing and tracing proceeds of crime in accordance with the provisions of chapter V of this Convention;

(*k*) The recovery of assets, in accordance with the provisions of chapter V of this Convention.

4. Without prejudice to domestic law, the competent authorities of a State Party may, without prior request, transmit information relating to criminal matters to a competent authority in another State Party where they believe that such information could assist the authority in undertaking or successfully concluding inquiries and criminal proceedings or could result in a request formulated by the latter State Party pursuant to this Convention.

5. The transmission of information pursuant to paragraph 4 of this article shall be without prejudice to inquiries and criminal proceedings in the
State of the competent authorities providing the information. The competent authorities receiving the information shall comply with a request that said information remain confidential, even temporarily, or with restrictions on its use. However, this shall not prevent the receiving State Party from disclosing in its proceedings information that is exculpatory to an accused person. In such a case, the receiving State Party shall notify the transmitting State Party prior to the disclosure and, if so requested, consult with the transmitting State Party. If, in an exceptional case, advance notice is not possible, the receiving State Party shall inform the transmitting State Party of the disclosure without delay.

6. The provisions of this article shall not affect the obligations under any other treaty, bilateral or multilateral, that governs or will govern, in whole or in part, mutual legal assistance.

7. Paragraphs 9 to 29 of this article shall apply to requests made pursuant to this article if the States Parties in question are not bound by a treaty of mutual legal assistance. If those States Parties are bound by such a treaty, the corresponding provisions of that treaty shall apply unless the States Parties agree to apply paragraphs 9 to 29 of this article in lieu thereof. States Parties are strongly encouraged to apply those paragraphs if they facilitate cooperation.

8. States Parties shall not decline to render mutual legal assistance pursuant to this article on the ground of bank secrecy.

9. (a) A requested State Party, in responding to a request for assistance pursuant to this article in the absence of dual criminality, shall take into account the purposes of this Convention, as set forth in article 1;

(b) States Parties may decline to render assistance pursuant to this article on the ground of absence of dual criminality. However, a requested State Party shall, where consistent with the basic concepts of its legal system, render assistance that does not involve coercive action. Such assistance may be refused when requests involve matters of a de minimis nature or matters for which the cooperation or assistance sought is available under other provisions of this Convention;

(c) Each State Party may consider adopting such measures as may be necessary to enable it to provide a wider scope of assistance pursuant to this article in the absence of dual criminality.

10. A person who is being detained or is serving a sentence in the territory of one State Party whose presence in another State Party is requested for purposes of identification, testimony or otherwise providing assistance in obtaining evidence for investigations, prosecutions or judicial proceedings in relation to offences covered by this Convention may be transferred if the following conditions are met:

(*a*) The person freely gives his or her informed consent;

(*b*) The competent authorities of both States Parties agree, subject to such conditions as those States Parties may deem appropriate.

11. For the purposes of paragraph 10 of this article:

(*a*) The State Party to which the person is transferred shall have the authority and obligation to keep the person transferred in custody, unless otherwise requested or authorized by the State Party from which the person was transferred;

(*b*) The State Party to which the person is transferred shall without delay implement its obligation to return the person to the custody of the State Party from which the person was transferred as agreed beforehand, or as otherwise agreed, by the competent authorities of both States Parties;

(*c*) The State Party to which the person is transferred shall not require the State Party from which the person was transferred to initiate extradition proceedings for the return of the person;

(*d*) The person transferred shall receive credit for service of the sentence being served in the State from which he or she was transferred for time spent in the custody of the State Party to which he or she was transferred.

12. Unless the State Party from which a person is to be transferred in accordance with paragraphs 10 and 11 of

this article so agrees, that person, whatever his or her nationality, shall not be prosecuted, detained, punished or subjected to any other restriction of his or her personal liberty in the territory of the State to which that person is transferred in respect of acts, omissions or convictions prior to his or her departure from the territory of the State from which he or she was transferred.

13. Each State Party shall designate a central authority that shall have the responsibility and power to receive requests for mutual legal assistance and either to execute them or to transmit them to the competent authorities for execution. Where a State Party has a special region or territory with a separate system of mutual legal assistance, it may designate a distinct central authority that shall have the same function for that region or territory. Central authorities shall ensure the speedy and proper execution or transmission of the requests received. Where the central authority transmits the request to a competent authority for execution, it shall encourage the speedy and proper execution of the request by the competent authority. The Secretary-General of the United Nations shall be notified of the central authority designated for this purpose at the time each State Party deposits its instrument of ratification, acceptance or approval of or accession to this Convention. Requests for mutual legal assistance and any communication related thereto shall be transmitted to the central authorities designated by the States Parties. This requirement shall be without prejudice to the right of a State Party to require that such requests and communications be addressed to it through diplomatic channels and, in urgent circumstances, where the States Parties agree, through the International Criminal Police Organization, if possible.

14. Requests shall be made in writing or, where possible, by any means capable of producing a written

record, in a language acceptable to the requested State Party, under conditions allowing that State Party to establish authenticity. The Secretary-General of the United Nations shall be notified of the language or languages acceptable to each State Party at the time it deposits its instrument of ratification, acceptance or approval of or accession to this Convention. In urgent circumstances and where agreed by the States Parties, requests may be made orally but shall be confirmed in writing forthwith.

15. A request for mutual legal assistance shall contain:

(*a*) The identity of the authority making the request;

(*b*) The subject matter and nature of the investigation, prosecution or judicial proceeding to which the request relates and the name and functions of the authority conducting the investigation, prosecution or judicial proceeding;

(*c*) A summary of the relevant facts, except in relation to requests for the purpose of service of judicial documents;

(*d*) A description of the assistance sought and details of any particular procedure that the requesting State Party wishes to be followed;

(*e*) Where possible, the identity, location and nationality of any person concerned; and

(*f*) The purpose for which the evidence, information or action is sought.

16. The requested State Party may request additional information when it appears necessary for the execution of the request in accordance with its domestic law or when it can facilitate such execution.

17. A request shall be executed in accordance with the domestic law of the requested State Party and, to the extent not contrary to the domestic law of the requested

State Party and where possible, in accordance with the procedures specified in the request.

18. Wherever possible and consistent with fundamental principles of domestic law, when an individual is in the territory of a State Party and has to be heard as a witness or expert by the judicial authorities of another State Party, the first State Party may, at the request of the other, permit the hearing to take place by video conference if it is not possible or desirable for the individual in question to appear in person in the territory of the requesting State Party. States Parties may agree that the hearing shall be conducted by a judicial authority of the requesting State Party and attended by a judicial authority of the requested State Party.

19. The requesting State Party shall not transmit or use information or evidence furnished by the requested State Party for investigations, prosecutions or judicial proceedings other than those stated in the request without the prior consent of the requested State Party. Nothing in this paragraph shall prevent the requesting State Party from disclosing in its proceedings information or evidence that is exculpatory to an accused person. In the latter case, the requesting State Party shall notify the requested State Party prior to the disclosure and, if so requested, consult with the requested State Party. If, in an exceptional case, advance notice is not possible, the requesting State Party shall inform the requested State Party of the disclosure without delay.

20. The requesting State Party may require that the requested State Party keep confidential the fact and substance of the request, except to the extent necessary to execute the request. If the requested State Party cannot comply with the requirement of confidentiality, it shall promptly inform the requesting State Party.

21. Mutual legal assistance may be refused:

(*a*) If the request is not made in conformity with the provisions of this article;

(*b*) If the requested State Party considers that execution of the request is likely to prejudice its sovereignty, security, ordre public or other essential interests;

(*c*) If the authorities of the requested State Party would be prohibited by its domestic law from carrying out the action requested with regard to any similar offence, had it been subject to investigation, prosecution or judicial proceedings under their own jurisdiction;

(*d*) If it would be contrary to the legal system of the requested State Party relating to mutual legal assistance for the request to be granted.

22. States Parties may not refuse a request for mutual legal assistance on the sole ground that the offence is also considered to involve fiscal matters.

23. Reasons shall be given for any refusal of mutual legal assistance.

24. The requested State Party shall execute the request for mutual legal assistance as soon as possible and shall take as full account as possible of any deadlines suggested by the requesting State Party and for which reasons are given, preferably in the request. The requesting State Party may make reasonable requests for information on the status and progress of measures taken by the requested State Party to satisfy its request. The requested State Party shall respond to reasonable requests by the requesting State Party on the status, and progress in its handling, of the request. The requesting State Party shall promptly inform the requested State Party when the assistance sought is no longer required.

25. Mutual legal assistance may be postponed by the requested State Party on the ground that it interferes with

an ongoing investigation, prosecution or judicial proceeding.

26. Before refusing a request pursuant to paragraph 21 of this article or postponing its execution pursuant to paragraph 25 of this article, the requested State Party shall consult with the requesting State Party to consider whether assistance may be granted subject to such terms and conditions as it deems necessary. If the requesting State Party accepts assistance subject to those conditions, it shall comply with the conditions.

27. Without prejudice to the application of paragraph 12 of this article, a witness, expert or other person who, at the request of the requesting State Party, consents to give evidence in a proceeding or to assist in an investigation, prosecution or judicial proceeding in the territory of the requesting State Party shall not be prosecuted, detained, punished or subjected to any other restriction of his or her personal liberty in that territory in respect of acts, omissions or convictions prior to his or her departure from the territory of the requested State Party. Such safe conduct shall cease when the witness, expert or other person having had, for a period of fifteen consecutive days or for any period agreed upon by the States Parties from the date on which he or she has been officially informed that his or her presence is no longer required by the judicial authorities, an opportunity of leaving, has nevertheless remained voluntarily in the territory of the requesting State Party or, having left it, has returned of his or her own free will.

28. The ordinary costs of executing a request shall be borne by the requested State Party, unless otherwise agreed by the States Parties concerned. If expenses of a substantial or extraordinary nature are or will be required to fulfil the request, the States Parties shall consult to determine the terms and conditions under which the

request will be executed, as well as the manner in which the costs shall be borne.

29. The requested State Party:

(a) Shall provide to the requesting State Party copies of government records, documents or information in its possession that under its domestic law are available to the general public;

(b) May, at its discretion, provide to the requesting State Party in whole, in part or subject to such conditions as it deems appropriate, copies of any government records, documents or information in its possession that under its domestic law are not available to the general public.

30. States Parties shall consider, as may be necessary, the possibility of concluding bilateral or multilateral agreements or arrangements that would serve the purposes of, give practical effect to or enhance the provisions of this article.

Article 47. *Transfer of criminal proceedings*

States Parties shall consider the possibility of transferring to one another proceedings for the prosecution of an offence established in accordance with this Convention in cases where such transfer is considered to be in the interests of the proper administration of justice, in particular in cases where several jurisdictions are involved, with a view to concentrating the prosecution.

Article 48. *Law enforcement cooperation*

1. States Parties shall cooperate closely with one another, consistent with their respective domestic legal and administrative systems, to enhance the effectiveness of law enforcement action to combat the offences covered by this Convention. States Parties shall, in particular, take effective measures:

(*a*) To enhance and, where necessary, to establish channels of communication between their competent authorities, agencies and services in order to facilitate the secure and rapid exchange of information concerning all aspects of the offences covered by this Convention, including, if the States Parties concerned deem it appropriate, links with other criminal activities;

(*b*) To cooperate with other States Parties in conducting inquiries with respect to offences covered by this Convention concerning: (i) The identity, whereabouts and activities of persons suspected of involvement in such offences or the location of other persons concerned; (ii) The movement of proceeds of crime or property derived from the commission of such offences; (iii) The movement of property, equipment or other instrumentalities used or intended for use in the commission of such offences;

(*c*) To provide, where appropriate, necessary items or quantities of substances for analytical or investigative purposes;

(*d*) To exchange, where appropriate, information with other States Parties concerning specific means and methods used to commit offences covered by this Convention, including the use of false identities, forged, altered or false documents and other means of concealing activities;

(*e*) To facilitate effective coordination between their competent authorities, agencies and services and to promote the exchange of personnel and other experts, including, subject to bilateral agreements or arrangements between the States Parties concerned, the posting of liaison officers;

(*f*) To exchange information and coordinate administrative and other measures taken as appropriate for the purpose of early identification of the offences covered by this Convention.

2. With a view to giving effect to this Convention, States Parties shall consider entering into bilateral or multilateral agreements or arrangements on direct cooperation between their law enforcement agencies and, where such agreements or arrangements already exist, amending them. In the absence of such agreements or arrangements between the States Parties concerned, the States Parties may consider this Convention to be the basis for mutual law enforcement cooperation in respect of the offences covered by this Convention. Whenever appropriate, States Parties shall make full use of agreements or arrangements, including international or regional organizations, to enhance the cooperation between their law enforcement agencies.

3. States Parties shall endeavour to cooperate within their means to respond to offences covered by this Convention committed through the use of modern technology.

Article 49. *Joint investigations*
States Parties shall consider concluding bilateral or multilateral agreements or arrangements whereby, in relation to matters that are the subject of investigations, prosecutions or judicial proceedings in one or more States, the competent authorities concerned may establish joint investigative bodies. In the absence of such agreements or arrangements, joint investigations may be undertaken by agreement on a case-by-case basis. The States Parties involved shall ensure that the sovereignty of the State Party in whose territory such investigation is to take place is fully respected.

Article 50. *Special investigative techniques*

1. In order to combat corruption effectively, each State Party shall, to the extent permitted by the basic principles

280

of its domestic legal system and in accordance with the conditions prescribed by its domestic law, take such measures as may be necessary, within its means, to allow for the appropriate use by its competent authorities of controlled delivery and, where it deems appropriate, other special investigative techniques, such as electronic or other forms of surveillance and undercover operations, within its territory, and to allow for the admissibility in court of evidence derived therefrom.

2. For the purpose of investigating the offences covered by this Convention, States Parties are encouraged to conclude, when necessary, appropriate bilateral or multilateral agreements or arrangements for using such special investigative techniques in the context of cooperation at the international level. Such agreements or arrangements shall be concluded and implemented in full compliance with the principle of sovereign equality of States and shall be carried out strictly in accordance with the terms of those agreements or arrangements.

3. In the absence of an agreement or arrangement as set forth in paragraph

2 of this article, decisions to use such special investigative techniques at the international level shall be made on a case-by-case basis and may, when necessary, take into consideration financial arrangements and understandings with respect to the exercise of jurisdiction by the States Parties concerned.

4. Decisions to use controlled delivery at the international level may, with the consent of the States Parties concerned, include methods such as intercepting and allowing the goods or funds to continue intact or be removed or replaced in whole or in part.

Chapter V
Asset recovery

Article 51. General provision

The return of assets pursuant to this chapter is a fundamental principle of this Convention, and States Parties shall afford one another the widest measure of cooperation and assistance in this regard.

Article 52. Prevention and detection of transfers of proceeds of crime

1. Without prejudice to article 14 of this Convention, each State Party shall take such measures as may be necessary, in accordance with its domestic law, to require financial institutions within its jurisdiction to verify the identity of customers, to take reasonable steps to determine the identity of beneficial owners of funds deposited into high-value accounts and to conduct enhanced scrutiny of accounts sought or maintained by or on behalf of individuals who are, or have been, entrusted with prominent public functions and their family members and close associates. S ɪch enhanced scrutiny shall be reasonably designed to detect suspicious transactions for the purpose of reporting to competent authorities and should not be so construed as to discourage or prohibit financial institutions from doing business with any legitimate customer.

2. In order to facilitate implementation of the measures provided for in paragraph 1 of this article, each State Party, in accordance with its domestic law and inspired by relevant initiatives of regional, interregional and multilateral organizations against money-laundering, shall:

(a) Issue advisories regarding the types of natural or

legal person to whose accounts financial institutions within its jurisdiction will be expected to apply enhanced scrutiny, the types of accounts and transactions to which to pay particular attention and appropriate account-opening, maintenance and recordkeeping measures to take concerning such accounts; and

(b) Where appropriate, notify financial institutions within its jurisdiction, at the request of another State Party or on its own initiative, of the identity of particular natural or legal persons to whose accounts such institutions will be expected to apply enhanced scrutiny, in addition to those whom the financial institutions may otherwise identify.

3. In the context of paragraph 2 (a) of this article, each State Party shall implement measures to ensure that its financial institutions maintain adequate records, over an appropriate period of time, of accounts and transactions involving the persons mentioned in paragraph 1 of this article, which should, as a minimum, contain information relating to the identity of the customer as well as, as far as possible, of the beneficial owner.

4. With the aim of preventing and detecting transfers of proceeds of offences established in accordance with this Convention, each State Party shall implement appropriate and effective measures to prevent, with the help of its regulatory and oversight bodies, the establishment of banks that have no physical presence and that are not affiliated with a regulated financial group. Moreover, States Parties may consider requiring their financial institutions to refuse to enter into or continue a correspondent banking relationship with such institutions and to guard against establishing relations with foreign financial institutions that permit their accounts to be used by banks that have no physical presence and that are not affiliated with a regulated financial group.

5. Each State Party shall consider establishing, in accordance with its domestic law, effective financial disclosure systems for appropriate public officials and shall provide for appropriate sanctions for non-compliance. Each State Party shall also consider taking such measures as may be necessary to permit its competent authorities to share that information with the competent authorities in other States Parties when necessary to investigate, claim and recover proceeds of offences established in accordance with this Convention.

6. Each State Party shall consider taking such measures as may be necessary, in accordance with its domestic law, to require appropriate public officials having an interest in or signature or other authority over a financial account in a foreign country to report that relationship to appropriate authorities and to maintain appropriate records related to such accounts. Such measures shall also provide for appropriate sanctions for non-compliance.

Article 53. Measures for direct recovery of property

Each State Party shall, in accordance with its domestic law:

(*a*) Take such measures as may be necessary to permit another State Party to initiate civil action in its courts to establish title to or ownership of property acquired through the commission of an offence established in accordance with this Convention;

(*b*) Take such measures as may be necessary to permit its courts to order those who have committed offences established in accordance with this Convention to pay compensation or damages to another State Party that has been harmed by such offences; and

(*c*) Take such measures as may be necessary to permit its courts or competent authorities, when having to decide on confiscation, to recognize another State Party's claim as a legitimate owner of property acquired through the commission of an offence established in accordance with this Convention.

Article 54. Mechanisms for recovery of property through international cooperation in confiscation

1. Each State Party, in order to provide mutual legal assistance pursuant to article 55 of this Convention with respect to property acquired through or involved in the commission of an offence established in accordance with this Convention, shall, in accordance with its domestic law:

(a) Take such measures as may be necessary to permit its competent authorities to give effect to an order of confiscation issued by a court of another State Party;

(b) Take such measures as may be necessary to permit its competent authorities, where they have jurisdiction, to order the confiscation of such property of foreign origin by adjudication of an offence of money-laundering or such other offence as may be within its jurisdiction or by other procedures authorized under its domestic law; and

(c) Consider taking such measures as may be necessary to allow confiscation of such property without a criminal conviction in cases in which the offender cannot be prosecuted by reason of death, flight or absence or in other appropriate cases.

2. Each State Party, in order to provide mutual legal assistance upon a request made pursuant to paragraph 2 of article 55 of this Convention, shall, in accordance with its domestic law:

(a) Take such measures as may be necessary to permit its competent authorities to freeze or seize property upon a freezing or seizure order issued by a court or competent authority of a requesting State Party that provides a reasonable basis for the requested State Party to believe that there are sufficient grounds for taking such actions and that the property would eventually be subject to an

order of confiscation for purposes of paragraph 1 (a) of this article;

(b) Take such measures as may be necessary to permit its competent authorities to freeze or seize property upon a request that provides a reasonable basis for the requested State Party to believe that there are sufficient grounds for taking such actions and that the property would eventually be subject to an order of confiscation for purposes of paragraph 1 (a) of this article; and

(c) Consider taking additional measures to permit its competent authorities to preserve property for confiscation, such as on the basis of a foreign arrest or criminal charge related to the acquisition of such property.

Article 55. International cooperation for purposes of confiscation

1. A State Party that has received a request from another State Party having jurisdiction over an offence established in accordance with this Convention for confiscation of proceeds of crime, property, equipment or other instrumentalities referred to in article 31, paragraph 1, of this Convention situated in its territory shall, to the greatest extent possible within its domestic legal system:

(a) Submit the request to its competent authorities for the purpose of obtaining an order of confiscation and, if such an order is granted, give effect to it; or

(b) Submit to its competent authorities, with a view to giving effect to it to the extent requested, an order of confiscation issued by a court in the territory of the requesting State Party in accordance with articles 31, paragraph 1, and 54, paragraph 1 (a), of this Convention insofar as it relates to proceeds of crime, property, equipment or other instrumentalities referred to in article 31, paragraph 1, situated in the territory of the requested State Party.

2. Following a request made by another State Party having jurisdiction over an offence established in accordance with this Convention, the requested State Party shall take measures to identify, trace and freeze or seize proceeds of crime, property, equipment or other instrumentalities referred to in article 31, paragraph 1, of this Convention for the purpose of eventual confiscation to be ordered either by the requesting State Party or, pursuant to a request under paragraph 1 of this article, by the requested State Party.

3. The provisions of article 46 of this Convention are applicable, mutatis mutandis, to this article. In addition to the information specified in article 46, paragraph 15, requests made pursuant to this article shall contain:

(a) In the case of a request pertaining to paragraph 1 (a) of this article, a description of the property to be confiscated, including, to the extent possible, the location and, where relevant, the estimated value of the property and a statement of the facts relied upon by the requesting State Party sufficient to enable the requested State Party to seek the order under its domestic law;

(b) In the case of a request pertaining to paragraph 1 (b) of this article, a legally admissible copy of an order of confiscation upon which the request is based issued by the requesting State Party, a statement of the facts and information as to the extent to which execution of the order is requested, a statement specifying the measures taken by the requesting State Party to provide adequate notification to bona fide third parties and to ensure due process and a statement that the confiscation order is final;

(c) In the case of a request pertaining to paragraph 2 of this article, a statement of the facts relied upon by the requesting State Party and a description of the actions requested and, where available, a legally admissible copy of an order on which the request is based.

4. The decisions or actions provided for in paragraphs 1 and 2 of this article shall be taken by the requested State Party in accordance with and subject to the provisions of its domestic law and its procedural rules or any bilateral or multilateral agreement or arrangement to which it may be bound in relation to the requesting State Party.

5. Each State Party shall furnish copies of its laws and regulations that give effect to this article and of any subsequent changes to such laws and regulations or a description thereof to the Secretary-General of the United Nations.

6. If a State Party elects to make the taking of the measures referred to in paragraphs 1 and 2 of this article conditional on the existence of a relevant treaty, that State Party shall consider this Convention the necessary and sufficient treaty basis.

7. Cooperation under this article may also be refused or provisional measures lifted if the requested State Party does not receive sufficient and timely evidence or if the property is of a de minimis value.

8. Before lifting any provisional measure taken pursuant to this article, the requested State Party shall, wherever possible, give the requesting State Party an opportunity to present its reasons in favour of continuing the measure.

9. The provisions of this article shall not be construed as prejudicing the rights of bona fide third parties.

Article 56. *Special cooperation*

Without prejudice to its domestic law, each State Party shall endeavour to take measures to permit it to forward, without prejudice to its own investigations, prosecutions or judicial proceedings, information on proceeds of offences established in accordance with this Convention to another State Party without prior request, when it considers that the disclosure of such information might assist the receiving State Party in initiating or carrying out investigations, prosecutions or judicial proceedings or might lead to a request by that State Party under this chapter of the Convention.

Article 57. Return and disposal of assets

1. Property confiscated by a State Party pursuant to article 31 or 55 of this Convention shall be disposed of, including by return to its prior legitimate owners, pursuant to paragraph 3 of this article, by that State Party in accordance with the provisions of this Convention and its domestic law.

2. Each State Party shall adopt such legislative and other measures, in accordance with the fundamental principles of its domestic law, as may be necessary to enable its competent authorities to return confiscated property, when acting on the request made by another State Party, in accordance with this Convention, taking into account the rights of bona fide third parties. 3. In accordance with articles 46 and 55 of this Convention and paragraphs 1 and 2 of this article, the requested State Party shall:

(a) In the case of embezzlement of public funds or of laundering of embezzled public funds as referred to in articles 17 and 23 of this Convention, when confiscation was executed in accordance with article 55 and on the basis of a final judgement in the requesting State Party, a requirement that can be waived by the requested State Party, return the confiscated property to the requesting State Party;

(b) In the case of proceeds of any other offence covered by this Convention, when the confiscation was executed in accordance with article 55 of this Convention and on the basis of a final judgement in the requesting State Party, a requirement that can be waived by the requested State Party, return the confiscated property to the requesting State Party, when the requesting State Party reasonably establishes its prior ownership of such confiscated property to the requested State Party or when the requested State Party recognizes damage to the requesting State Party as a basis for returning the confiscated property;

(c) In all other cases, give priority consideration to returning confiscated property to the requesting State Party, returning such property to its prior legitimate owners or compensating the victims of the crime.

4. Where appropriate, unless States Parties decide otherwise, the requested State Party may deduct reasonable expenses incurred in investigations, prosecutions or judicial proceedings leading to the return or disposition of confiscated property pursuant to this article.

5. Where appropriate, States Parties may also give special consideration to concluding agreements or mutually acceptable arrangements, on a case-bycase basis, for the final disposal of confiscated property.

Article 58. Financial intelligence unit

States Parties shall cooperate with one another for the purpose of preventing and combating the transfer of proceeds of offences established in accordance with this Convention and of promoting ways and means of recovering such proceeds and, to that end, shall consider establishing a financial intelligence unit to be responsible for receiving, analysing and disseminating to the competent authorities reports of suspicious financial transactions.

Article 59. *Bilateral and multilateral agreements and arrangements*

States Parties shall consider concluding bilateral or multilateral agreements or arrangements to enhance the effectiveness of international cooperation undertaken pursuant to this chapter of the Convention.

Chapter VI
Technical assistance and information exchange

Article 60. *Training and technical assistance*

1. Each State Party shall, to the extent necessary, initiate, develop or improve specific training programmes for its personnel responsible for preventing and combating corruption. Such training programmes could deal, inter alia, with the following areas:

(a) Effective measures to prevent, detect, investigate, punish and control corruption, including the use of evidence-gathering and investigative methods;

(b) Building capacity in the development and planning of strategic anticorruption policy;

(c) Training competent authorities in the preparation of requests for mutual legal assistance that meet the requirements of this Convention;

(d) Evaluation and strengthening of institutions, public service management and the management of public finances, including public procurement, and the private sector;

(e) Preventing and combating the transfer of proceeds of offences established in accordance with this Convention and recovering such proceeds;

(f) Detecting and freezing of the transfer of proceeds of offences established in accordance with this Convention;

(g) Surveillance of the movement of proceeds of offences established in accordance with this Convention and of the methods used to transfer, conceal or disguise such proceeds;

(h) Appropriate and efficient legal and administrative mechanisms and methods for facilitating the return of proceeds of offences established in accordance with this Convention;

(i) Methods used in protecting victims and witnesses who cooperate with judicial authorities; and

(j) Training in national and international regulations and in languages.

2. States Parties shall, according to their capacity, consider affording one another the widest measure of technical assistance, especially for the benefit of developing countries, in their respective plans and programmes to combat corruption, including material support and training in the areas referred to in paragraph 1 of this article, and training and assistance and the mutual exchange of relevant experience and specialized knowledge, which will facilitate international cooperation between States Parties in the areas of extradition and mutual legal assistance.

3. States Parties shall strengthen, to the extent necessary, efforts to maximize operational and training activities in international and regional organizations and in the framework of relevant bilateral and multilateral agreements or arrangements.

4. States Parties shall consider assisting one another, upon request, in conducting evaluations, studies and research relating to the types, causes, effects and costs of corruption in their respective countries, with a view to developing, with the participation of competent authorities and society, strategies and action plans to combat corruption.

5. In order to facilitate the recovery of proceeds of offences established in accordance with this Convention, States Parties may cooperate in providing each other with the names of experts who could assist in achieving that objective.

6. States Parties shall consider using subregional, regional and international conferences and seminars to promote cooperation and technical assistance and to stimulate discussion on problems of mutual concern, including the special problems and needs of developing countries and countries with economies in transition.

7. States Parties shall consider establishing voluntary mechanisms with a view to contributing financially to the efforts of developing countries and countries with economies in transition to apply this Convention through technical assistance programmes and projects.

8. Each State Party shall consider making voluntary contributions to the United Nations Office on Drugs and Crime for the purpose of fostering, through the Office, programmes and projects in developing countries with a view to implementing this Convention.

Article 61. Collection, exchange and analysis of information on corruption

1. Each State Party shall consider analysing, in consultation with experts, trends in corruption in its territory, as well as the circumstances in which corruption offences are committed.

2. States Parties shall consider developing and sharing with each other and through international and regional organizations statistics, analytical expertise concerning corruption and information with a view to developing, insofar as possible, common definitions, standards and methodologies, as well as information on best practices to prevent and combat corruption.

3. Each State Party shall consider monitoring its policies and actual measures to combat corruption and making assessments of their effectiveness and efficiency.

Article 62. Other measures: implementation of the Convention through economic development and technical assistance

1. States Parties shall take measures conducive to the optimal implementation of this Convention to the extent possible, through international cooperation, taking into account the negative effects of corruption on society in general, in particular on sustainable development.

2. States Parties shall make concrete efforts to the extent possible and in coordination with each other, as well as with international and regional organizations:

(*a*) To enhance their cooperation at various levels with developing countries, with a view to strengthening the capacity of the latter to prevent and combat corruption;

(*b*) To enhance financial and material assistance to support the efforts of developing countries to prevent and fight corruption effectively and to help them implement this Convention successfully;

(*c*) To provide technical assistance to developing countries and countries with economies in transition to assist them in meeting their needs for the implementation of this Convention. To that end, States Parties shall endeavour to make adequate and regular voluntary contributions to an account specifically designated for that purpose in a United Nations funding mechanism. States Parties may also give special consideration, in accordance with their domestic law and the provisions of this Convention, to contributing to that account a percentage of the money or of the corresponding value of proceeds of crime or property confiscated in accordance with the provisions of this Convention;

(d) To encourage and persuade other States and financial institutions as appropriate to join them in efforts in accordance with this article, in particular by providing more training programmes and modern equipment to developing countries in order to assist them in achieving the objectives of this Convention.

3. To the extent possible, these measures shall be without prejudice to existing foreign assistance commitments or to other financial cooperation arrangements at the bilateral, regional or international level.

4. States Parties may conclude bilateral or multilateral agreements or arrangements on material and logistical assistance, taking into consideration the financial arrangements necessary for the means of international cooperation provided for by this Convention to be effective and for the prevention, detection and control of corruption.

Chapter VII
Mechanisms for implementation

Article 63. Conference of the States Parties to the Convention

1. A Conference of the States Parties to the Convention is hereby established to improve the capacity of and cooperation between States Parties to achieve the objectives set forth in this Convention and to promote and review its implementation.

2. The Secretary-General of the United Nations shall convene the Conference of the States Parties not later than

one year following the entry into force of this Convention. Thereafter, regular meetings of the Conference of the States Parties shall be held in accordance with the rules of procedure adopted by the Conference.

3. The Conference of the States Parties shall adopt rules of procedure and rules governing the functioning of the activities set forth in this article, including rules concerning the admission and participation of observers, and the payment of expenses incurred in carrying out those activities.

4. The Conference of the States Parties shall agree upon activities, procedures
and methods of work to achieve the objectives set forth in paragraph 1 of this article, including:

(a) Facilitating activities by States Parties under articles 60 and 62 and chapters II to V of this Convention, including by encouraging the mobilization of voluntary contributions;

(b) Facilitating the exchange of information among States Parties on patterns and trends in corruption and on successful practices for preventing and combating it and for the return of proceeds of crime, through, inter alia, the publication of relevant information as mentioned in this article;

(c) Cooperating with relevant international and regional organizations and mechanisms and non-governmental organizations;

(d) Making appropriate use of relevant information produced by other international and regional mechanisms for combating and preventing corruption in order to avoid unnecessary duplication of work;

(e) Reviewing periodically the implementation of this Convention by its States Parties;

(f) Making recommendations to improve this Convention and its implementation;

(g) Taking note of the technical assistance requirements of States Parties with regard to the implementation of this Convention and recommending any action it may deem necessary in that respect.

5. For the purpose of paragraph 4 of this article, the Conference of the States Parties shall acquire the necessary knowledge of the measures taken by States Parties in implementing this Convention and the difficulties encountered by them in doing so through information provided by them and through such supplemental review mechanisms as may be established by the Conference of the States Parties.

6. Each State Party shall provide the Conference of the States Parties with information on its programmes, plans and practices, as well as on legislative and administrative measures to implement this Convention, as required by the Conference of the States Parties. The Conference of the States Parties shall examine the most effective way of receiving and acting upon information, including, inter alia, information received from States Parties and from competent international organizations. Inputs received from relevant non-governmental organizations duly accredited in accordance with procedures to be decided upon by the Conference of the States Parties may also be considered.

7. Pursuant to paragraphs 4 to 6 of this article, the Conference of the States Parties shall establish, if it deems it necessary, any appropriate mechanism or body to assist in the effective implementation of the Convention.

Article 64. Secretariat

1. The Secretary-General of the United Nations shall provide the necessary secretariat services to the Conference of the States Parties to the Convention.

2. The secretariat shall:

(*a*) Assist the Conference of the States Parties in carrying out the activities set forth in article 63 of this Convention and make arrangements and provide the necessary services for the sessions of the Conference of the States Parties;

(*b*) Upon request, assist States Parties in providing information to the Conference of the States Parties as envisaged in article 63, paragraphs 5 and 6, of this Convention; and

(*c*) Ensure the necessary coordination with the secretariats of relevant international and regional organizations.

Chapter VIII
Final provisions

Article 65. *Implementation of the Convention*

1. Each State Party shall take the necessary measures, including legislative and administrative measures, in accordance with fundamental principles of its domestic law, to ensure the implementation of its obligations under this Convention.

2. Each State Party may adopt more strict or severe measures than those provided for by this Convention for preventing and combating corruption.

Article 66. *Settlement of disputes*

1. States Parties shall endeavour to settle disputes concerning the interpretation or application of this Convention through negotiation.

2. Any dispute between two or more States Parties concerning the interpretation or application of this Convention that cannot be settled through negotiation within a reasonable time shall, at the request of one of those States Parties, be submitted to arbitration. If, six months after the date of the request for arbitration, those States Parties are unable to agree on the organization of the arbitration, any one of those States Parties may refer the dispute to the International Court of Justice by request in accordance with the Statute of the Court.

3. Each State Party may, at the time of signature, ratification, acceptance or approval of or accession to this Convention, declare that it does not consider itself bound by paragraph 2 of this article. The other States Parties shall not be bound by paragraph 2 of this article with respect to any State Party that has made such a reservation.

4. Any State Party that has made a reservation in accordance with paragraph

3 of this article may at any time withdraw that reservation by notification to the Secretary-General of the United Nations.

Article 67. Signature, ratification, acceptance, approval and accession

1. This Convention shall be open to all States for signature from 9 to 11 December 2003 in Merida, Mexico, and thereafter at United Nations Headquarters in New York until 9 December 2005.

2. This Convention shall also be open for signature by regional economic integration organizations provided that at least one member State of such organization has signed this Convention in accordance with paragraph 1 of this article.

3. This Convention is subject to ratification, acceptance or approval. Instruments of ratification, acceptance or approval shall be deposited with the Secretary-General of the United Nations. A regional economic integration organization may deposit its instrument of ratification, acceptance or approval if at least one of its member States has done likewise. In that instrument of ratification, acceptance or approval, such organization shall declare the extent of its competence with respect to the matters governed by this Convention. Such organization shall also inform the depositary of any relevant modification in the extent of its competence.

4. This Convention is open for accession by any State or any regional economic integration organization of which at least one member State is a Party to this Convention. Instruments of accession shall be deposited with the Secretary-General of the United Nations. At the time of its accession, a regional economic integration organization shall declare the extent of its competence with respect to matters governed by this Convention. Such organization shall also inform the depositary of any relevant modification in the extent of its competence.

Article 68. Entry into force

1. This Convention shall enter into force on the ninetieth day after the date of deposit of the thirtieth instrument of ratification, acceptance, approval or accession. For the purpose of this paragraph, any instrument deposited by a regional economic integration organization shall not be counted as additional to those deposited by member States of such organization.

2. For each State or regional economic integration organization ratifying, accepting, approving or acceding to this Convention after the deposit of the thirtieth instrument of such action, this Convention shall enter into

force on the thirtieth day after the date of deposit by such State or organization of the relevant instrument or on the date this Convention enters into force pursuant to paragraph 1 of this article, whichever is later.

Article 69. *Amendment*

1. After the expiry of five years from the entry into force of this Convention, a State Party may propose an amendment and transmit it to the Secretary-General of the United Nations, who shall thereupon communicate the proposed amendment to the States Parties and to the Conference of the States Parties to the Convention for the purpose of considering and deciding on the proposal. The Conference of the States Parties shall make every effort to achieve consensus on each amendment. If all efforts at consensus·have been exhausted and no agreement has been reached, the amendment shall, as a last resort, require for its adoption a two-thirds majority vote of the States Parties present and voting at the meeting of the Conference of the States Parties.

2. Regional economic integration organizations, in matters within their competence, shall exercise their right to vote under this article with a number of votes equal to the number of their member States that are Parties to this Convention. Such organizations shall not exercise their right to vote if their member States exercise theirs and vice versa.

3. An amendment adopted in accordance with paragraph 1 of this article is subject· to ratification, acceptance or approval by States Parties.

4. An amendment adopted in accordance with paragraph 1 of this article shall enter into force in respect of a State Party ninety days after the date of the deposit with the Secretary-General of the United Nations·of an

instrument of ratification, acceptance or approval of such amendment.

5. When an amendment enters into force, it shall be binding on those States Parties which have expressed their consent to be bound by it. Other States Parties shall still be bound by the provisions of this Convention and any earlier amendments that they have ratified, accepted or approved.

Article 70. *Denunciation*

1. A State Party may denounce this Convention by written notification to the Secretary-General of the United Nations. Such denunciation shall become effective one year after the date of receipt of the notification by the Secretary-General.

2. A regional economic integration organization shall cease to be a Party to this Convention when all of its member States have denounced it.

Article 71. *Depositary and languages*

1. The Secretary-General of the United Nations is designated depositary of this Convention.

2. The original of this Convention, of which the Arabic, Chinese, English, French, Russian and Spanish texts are equally authentic, shall be deposited with the Secretary-General of the United Nations.

IN WITNESS WHEREOF, the undersigned plenipotentiaries, being duly authorized thereto by their respective Governments, have signed this Convention.

Bibliography

- Bible de Jérusalem, Cerf, Verbum Bible, 1995.
- La Bible expliquée et commentée, Alliance Biblique universelle.
- Concile œcuménique Vatican II, Centurion, Paris, 1967.
- La liturgie des heures, tome 1-2-3, Cerf - Desclée de Brouwer - Mame, Paris, 1998.

MAIN BOOKS

1. Abéga, Séverin Cécile, Société civile et réduction de la pauvreté, Clé, Yaoundé, 1999.
2. Alt Eric et Irène Luc, Lutte contre la corruption, Paris, PUF, 1997.
3. Arendt Hannah, Du mensonge à la violence, Paris, Calmann-Levy, 1989.
4. Arendt Hannah, La crise de la Culture, Paris, Gallimard, 1972.
5. Lucien Ayissi, Corruption et gouvernance, Yaoundé, PUY, 2003.
6. Lucien Ayissi, Corruption et pauvreté, Paris, L'Harmattan, 2007.
7. Lucien Ayissi, Gouvernance camerounaise et lutte contre la pauvreté. Interpellations éthiques et propositions politiques, Paris, L'Harmattan, 2009.
8. Lucien Ayissi, La prière de Yakop, Paris, L'Harmattan, 2010.
9. Blundo G. et Olivier de Sardan, État et corruption en Afrique, Une anthropologie comparative des relations entre fonctionnaires et usagers (Bénin, Niger, Sénégal), Paris, Karthala, 2007.
10. Dobel J. Patrick, Intégrité morale et vie publique, Nouveaux Horizons-ARS, Paris, 2003.
11. Dommel Daniel, Face à la corruption, Paris Karthala, 2003.
12. Elwell Walter, Le Petit Guide de la Bible, Forel, Maine-la-Vallée, 1984.
13. Foucault Michel, Dits et Écrits, Vol 4, Paris, Gallimard, 2001.
14. Foulquié Paul, Dictionnaire de la langue philosophique, Paris, 6e édition, PUF.
15. Grant Georges, The Changing of the de Guard, Broadman & Holman Nashville, Tennessee, 1995, 1995.
16. Havel Vaclav, L'angoisse de la liberté, Paris, Editions de l'Aube, 1994.
17. Hugo, V., Les Misérables 1 et 2, Livre de poche, Paris, 1998.
18. Humbrecht Thierry-Dominique, Théologie négative et noms divins chez Saint THomas d'Aquin, J. Vrin, Paris, 2005.
19. Kant Emmanuel, Critique de la raison pure, Paris, PUF, 1984, 584p.
20. Robert Klitgaard, Combattre la corruption, Nouveaux horizons, ARS, Paris.
21. Robert Klitgaard et als, Villes corrompues. Du diagnostic aux remèdes, Nouveaux horizons, ARS, Paris, 2002.
22. Nwel Titi Pierre (Sous la dir.), De la corruption au Cameroun, Saagraph, Yaoundé, 1999.

23. Peeters Marguerite A., *La Mondialisation de la révolution de la culture occidentale. Concepts-clefs, Mécanisme opérationnels*, Bruxelles, Institute for Intercultural Dialogue Dynamics, 2007.
24. Regis Jolivet, *Manuel de philosophie*, Emmanuel Vitte, Lyon-Paris, 4è éd. n° 1348.
25. Sikounmo Hilaire, *L'école du sous-développement. Gros plan sur l'enseignement secondaire en Afrique*, L'Harmattan, Paris, 1992.
26. Thierry-Dominique Humbrecht, *Théologie négative et noms divins* chez Saint THomas d'Aquin, J. Vrin, Paris, 2005.
27. Vallée Olivier, *La police morale de l'anticorruption*, Karthala, Cameroun, Nigeria, Paris, 2010.
28. Victor Hugo, *Les misérables 1*, Livres de Poches, Paris, 1998.
29. Jean-Emmanuel Pondi, *Harcèlement sexuel et déontologie en milieu universitaire*, Yaoundé, Clé, 2011.

DICTIONAIRIES

- *Dictionnaire culturel du christianisme*, Paris, Nathan, 1994.
- *Dictionnaire encyclopédique de l'écologie et des sciences de l'Environnement*, Paris, Ediscience, 1993.
- Le Petit Robert, *Dictionnaire alphabétique et analogique de la langue française*, Les Dictionnaires ROBER-CANADA, Montréal, 1992.
- *Petit dictionnaire de la Bible*, Verbum Bible, Forel, Marne-La vallée, 1996.
- Droguet & Ardant, *Nouvelle Encyclopédie catholique Théo,* Paris Fayard, 1989.

FILES

- *Transparency International, Combattre la corruption. Enjeux et perspectives*, Karthala, Paris, 2002.
- *Transparency International, Rapport mondial sur la corruption 2003, Thème spécial : L'accès à l'information,* Karthala, Paris.
- *Transparency International, Rapport mondial sur la corruption 2004, Thème spécial : La corruption politique,* Karthala, Paris.
- *Transparency International, Rapport mondial sur la corruption 2005, Thème spécial : Corruption dans le secteur de la construction et la reconstruction d'après- guerre*, Economica, Paris.
- *Transparency International, Rapport mondial sur la corruption 2006, Thème spécial : Corruption et santé*, Karthala, Paris.

NEWS PAPERS/REVIEWS

- *Abbia*, Fonlon Bernard, Construire ou Détruire, Yaoundé, Clé, 1964.
- *Germinal*, n° 058, du 10 juin 2010.
- *Le messager*, n°2403, du 5/07/2007.
- *Le Messager*, n°2470, du 04/10/2007.

Macacos - Imprimerie leader - N°0017132
Dépôt légal 1ᵉʳ tirage : Août 2011
Printed in Macacos - Douala (Cameroon)